I
LOVE
FUTURA

I Love Type Series
Volume One

Published
by Viction:ary

Edited & Designed
by TwoPoints.Net

JEDER DRUCKER

SUCHT nach einer guten Schrift die dem Stilwillen unserer Zeit entspricht, die gut lesbar und schön ist

HIER IST SIE!

Um die Verwendungs-Möglichkeiten der
FUTURA
zu erhöhen, schnitten wir neben dieser
ersten Form des r
noch ein zweites r

Kraftsport-Verein Trier
Die drei Grenadiere
Der Frankfurter Hof
Führer durch Worms
Reit-Turnier
Freimarke

BAUERSCHE GIESSEREI
FRANKFURT A. M. · BARCELONA · NEW YORK

¡FU-TU-RA!
El FU-tipo más
FU-imitado
desde los
FU-tiempos
de FU-Gutenberg
FU —— P.D.:
¡El tipo más vendido!
¡FU —— IN!

A B C D E F G H I J K L M N Ñ O P Q R
S T U V W X Y Z
a b c d e f g h i j k l m n ñ o p q r s t
u v w x y z

PRADILLA · fortuny · pradilla
FORTUNY · pradilla · fortuny
ZULOAGA · nonell · zuloaga
NONELL · zuloaga · nonell

Se dió por formar inscripciones figurativas o idiográficas donde el sol era representado por un círculo y la vigilancia por un ojo

When in 1927 the Bauersche Giesserei introduced the first weights cast in lead of its new typeface Futura, very few people could imagine that the sentence, with which the German typefoundry described the type, would keep its validity until nowadays... reaching soon its 100 years of existence.

Paul Renner (1878–1956), the designer of Futura, showed the first sketches of the alphabet to my grandfather, Georg Hartmann, owner of the Bauersche Giesserei, thanks to the intermediation of Heinrich Jost, Art Director of the Foundry and former student of Renner. The typeface aroused immediately Hartmann's enthusiasm; it was a great breakthrough in its time. The originality of its design consisted in its geometric forms, based on the circle, the triangle and the square; however the outline of the circles was slightly oval in order to make reading easier. The whole alphabet was conceived with a functional aim, an effectiveness that eliminated all that could look "calligraphic" or decorative. This simplicity responded to the trends of the era in the arts, architecture or painting, the Bauhaus or constructivism; therefore still valid in our current era of minimalism.

To convert the sketches of the alphabet to letters cast in lead, ready for sale, exactly three years had to pass: from 1924 to 1927. This long period of elaboration can be partly understood due to the complexity of the process of manufacturing the first letters in lead, from engraving the patterns and the matrices to the adjustments in the casting machine. The complete alphabet for one sole size for one sole weight required the engraving of some 120 matrices—small caps, caps, vowels with accents, numbers and punctuation. Furthermore, every size from 5 to 84 point required almost the same number of matrices.

But most of all, the delay in finishing Futura for its introduction into the market was due to the great care brought to the execution of its final forms. Many letters that were initially designed were later rejected. The skill of the engravers, the frequent improvements required by the Art Director Heinrich Jost, and finally the strictness as well as the patience which the owner of the foundry Georg Hartmann showed during the whole long process of manufacturing, contributed to the great success of Futura from a very beginning.

The fast introduction of Futura at a global level can be mainly explained due to the company's structure. The Bauersche Giesserei used to be the typefoundry with the largest capacity of production in Germany, after the absorption of various typefoundries in the country during World War I and the postwar period. It disposed of a dynamic network of distributors in the neighboring countries. In Spain it used to operate the typefoundry Neufville, directed since 1923 by my father Carlos Hartmann. From Neufville the types were exported to Portugal and Latin America. In the US a subsidiary company was established—firstly under the name of the Bauer Typefoundry but later changed to Bauer Alphabets—and was the main provider of European types in America. The prestige of these companies was not only based on the fact of offering a type as unique as Futura but also due to other typefaces of great reputation such as Bauer Bodoni, Weiss, Schneidler, Corvinus, Bernhard, Menhart... alphabets designed by German, Czech, Hungarian or American artists.

Futura was not a typeface produced only by the company group directed by Georg Hartmann. In the 1930s, the typefoundry Deberny & Peignot signed an agreement with the Bauersche Giesserei for the casting and selling of Futura exclusively for the French market. D&P changed the name Futura to "Europe" and with this name became the most popular typeface in France. In Argentina, the sales agents Serra Hermanos, long time distributors of Bauer types, requested the license to manufacture Futura just a few years after World War II. They had bought a typefoundry with the aim to sell their own Futura to the South American countries.

In the late fifties of the previous century, just before the appearance of photocomposition, which would convulse the typefoundry field, the Bauersche Giesserei and its sister-company in Barcelona would find themselves in an absolutely extraordinary situation. The casting machines that both companies had installed could not cope with the necessary production to respond to the great demand of printing types requested by printers all over the world. As a matter of fact it was Futura that they wished to buy, since 75% of the sales of Bauer focused in this typeface. So the decision was taken to offer the casting of Futura for the Anglo-American market to the English typefoundry Stephenson & Blake. For this purpose Stephenson & Blake had to re-engrave the matrices of various sizes and weights of Futura; it was a truly important investment to increase the production of types cast in Pica System.

We have seen that the unprecedented success of Futura drove the Bauersche Giesserei to the decision to outsource its production to typefoundries situated in different countries, a fact that had never occurred before in the history of Graphic Arts. For this reason Futura could reach a great popularity in all countries over the world at the same time, hence converting itself in the most highly regarded typeface amongst printers of all nationalities. What was left to define was the company's strategy to allow manufacturers of composition machines to have Futura in their program.

When Georg Hartmann acquired the Bauersche Giesserei in 1898, Mergenthaler had invented the machine to cast lines of types, enabling text to be typeset in a much shorter time than it could be set by hand. The sale of these machines contributed to the disappearance of many typefoundries. Therefore Linotype seemed to be a competitor and any alliances had to be avoided. Moreover, the Bauersche Giesserei's main competitor, Stempel AG, also from Frankfurt, had permitted, even before World War II, the US Mergenthaler Company to become its first share holder and have therefore in exchange the opportunity to produce matrices for the Linotype machines.

Due to these circumstances, it took long for the Bauersche Giesserei to provide the availability of Futura for the photocomposing machine. It did so, when the market conditions demanded that a type such as Futura—in order to assure its success—could be supplied simultaneously in both manual and mechanical composition. Therefore a deal with Intertype—Linotype's major competitor—was signed. For a long time Intertype was the only supplier of the matrices of Futura to printers. Finally Linotype joined the deal after realizing that the sales of Futura matrices was good business.

In the late 1950s, the photocomposing machines burst in the market and precipitated the end of the typefoundries. The manufacturers of composing machines of types in lead, like Linotype and Monotype, adapted their machinery to new technology and other typefoundries like Deberny & Peignot had either entered a collaboration with a new manufacturer or developed their own photocomposition machines, as Berthold did. The typefaces of these foundries were manufactured in an exclusive way for the corresponding systems of photocomposing. These machines were "closed systems", in other words the image carriers could not be used with another system. While the sales of machinery was converted into the main goal of these companies, typefaces like the ones of Stempel/Linotype were only available in the photocomposing machines of Linotype.

The Bauersche Giesserei preferred not to diversify its activities in their own manufacturing of photocomposing machines. We know "a posteriori", that this decision was correct, since the era of photocomposition was extremely short and furthermore the new technological change with the step towards the digital age put these manufacturers in serious financial difficulties.

Therefore, the Bauersche Giesserei, free of engagements with manufacturers of matrices and machines, decided to cede its typefaces to third parties under license. By this way, Futura would soon be available in the closed systems of photocomposition of Linotype, Monotype, Photon, Berthold, Bobst and many others, as well as in the very popular in those years Letraset transfer sheets. Despite the great care manufacturers had put in that their version were the most accurate adaptation of the original, some slight differences could be noticed between one Futura version and another; mostly due to the fact that every company "interpreted" the forms of Futura in their way.

The transition from the manual composition in lead and typographic printing to photocomposition and offset printing obliged the Bauersche Giesserei—as well as many other typefoundries—to close down. In 1972 the company sold the international rights over their typefaces—particularly the Futura ones—to the Spanish family branch Fundición Tipográfica Neufville, SA. Neufville continued with the strategy to license its typefaces, up to 1995 when it changed to "Bauer Types", which still maintains its active presence in the international scene. Furthermore, the company continues to be owned by the Hartmann family, a rather unusual fact for this activity in such convulsive times.

Once the digital technology was introduced in the graphic world, Bauer Types would cede the rights of the making of Futura to Adobe, Apple, Berthold, Bitstream, Elsner & Flake, Linotype, Monotype, Paratype, URW++, Wiescher. These manufacturers sell Futura directly to the users or through distributors like MyFonts, FontShop, FontHaus and others.

In 1997 Bauer Types signed a deal with Visualogik creating the software of Bauer's typefaces. Visualogik, a leading Dutch company in the development of font software, digitized the different weights of Futura by working with the original letters cast in lead. These weights are available under the name of Futura ND, as the initials ND mean "Neufville Digital", the joint venture of Bauer and Visualogik.

Futura ND is available in 36 weights, including small caps, old style figures and ligatures, all identical to the originals designed by Paul Renner; in other words, the most complete Futura of all versions available up to date.

Now Futura continues to be a typeface of universal use and available almost everywhere, exactly as Georg Hartmann made available the types in lead cast in different locations. Also, the sentence "Futura: the typeface of today and of tomorrow" still remains powerful. The world is changing, but Futura always remains present, it is the favorite of every period of time.

Wolfgang Hartmann
Bauer Types

Typeface In Use
Customized Futura Medium

"The typeface's simple, geometric style, in contrast to the fun, figurative shapes give the right playful expression, referring to the old Folk Park aesthetics."

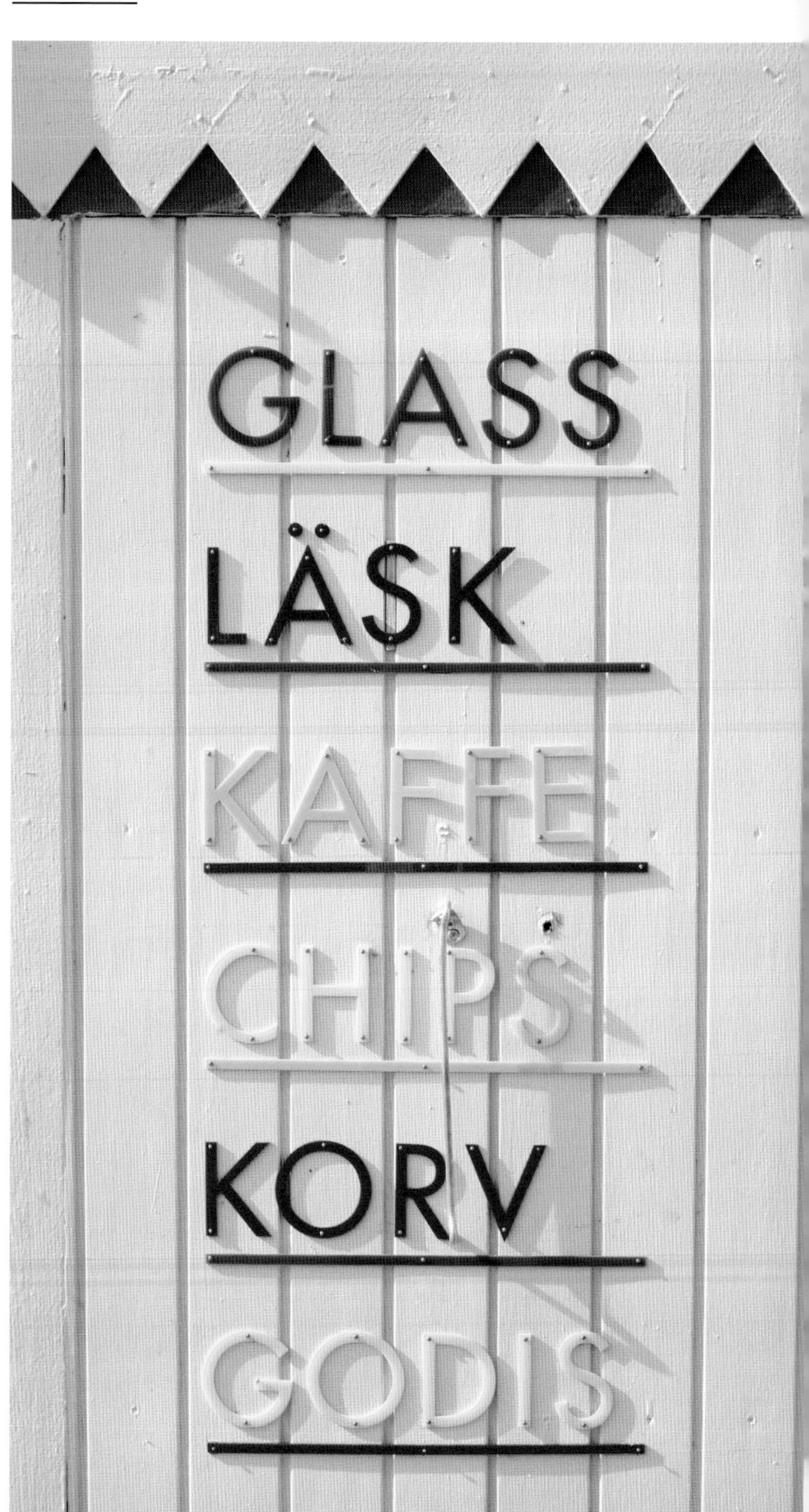

Folkets Park
2009 – Typography concept for signage in the amusement park Folkets Park, Malmö, Sweden
Client Folkets Park, Malmö, Sweden
Design Byggstudio

The typography illustrates the range of activities available in the park and the fun and entertaining nature of the features there—the kiosks, the mini-golf, the kid's zoo, the Rose sculpture and the Ferris wheel. The letters are laser-cut in acrylic and partly magnetic which makes it possible to change the menu signs during the season. This also presents further opportunity for creative and imaginative variation.

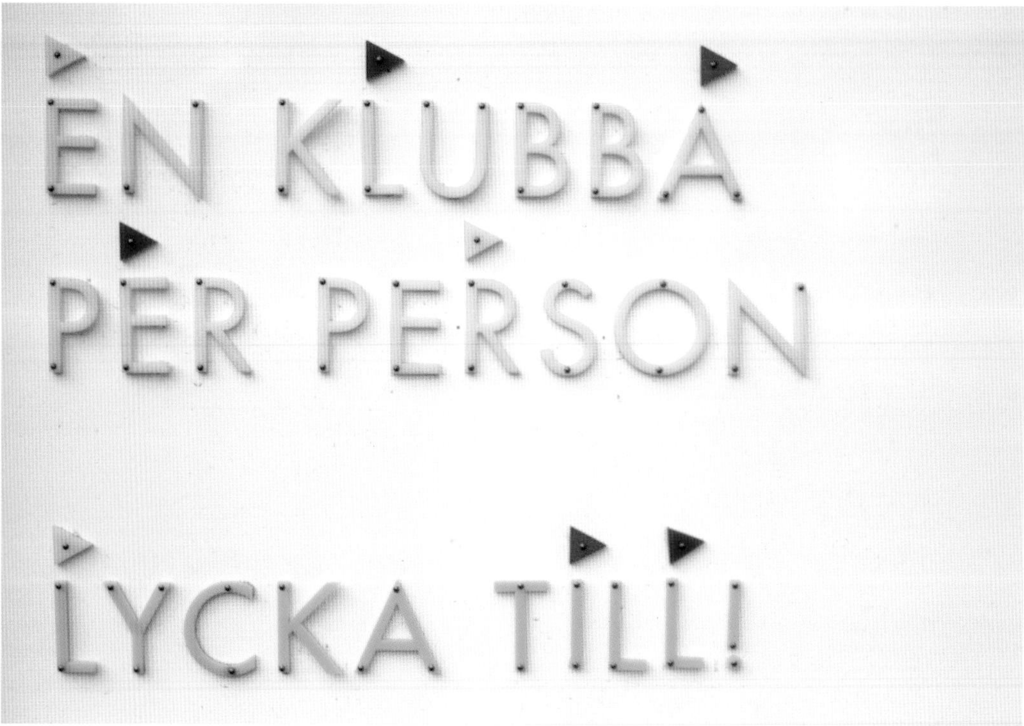
EN KLUBBA
PER PERSON
LYCKA TILL!

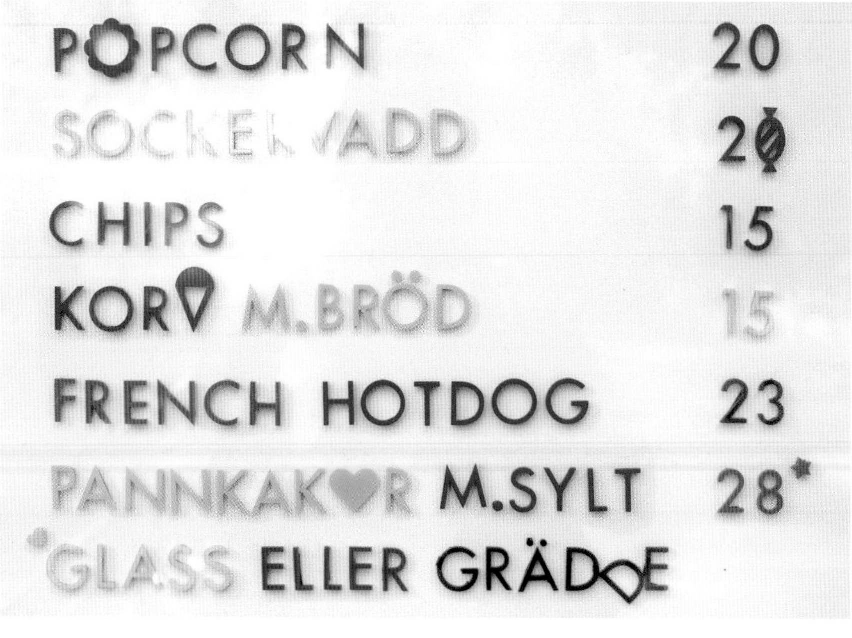
POPCORN 20
SOCKERVADD 20
CHIPS 15
KORV M.BRÖD 15
FRENCH HOTDOG 23
PANNKAKOR M.SYLT 28*
*GLASS ELLER GRÄDDE

Byggstudio's Favorite Futura Letter Is 'Q'.

Iconic Album Covers
2010 – Packaging
Client Institute of Contemporary Art, London
Design Studio Astrid Stavro

The ICA asked us to design six CD/DVD labels and the matching six sleeves for Sixpak as well as the graphics for the packaging. We developed a series of CD/DVD sleeves that typographically recreate iconic album covers. These covers transcend their original context to become key cultural concepts, which insinuate themselves deeper into our shared, collective memory. We all know them. They come to the mind's eye with just a mention of it. What is it that makes these covers stick in the mind, while others quickly fade? Certain album covers become unforgettable because they define specific moments that are a part of our common culture. They have become part of a visual vocabulary in a world where we increasingly communicate by using pictures rather than words. What they have in common is that we all have them in common. The series are a cultural, historic homage as well as a fun trivia game.

"I was looking for a neutral, legible, clean and modern feel."

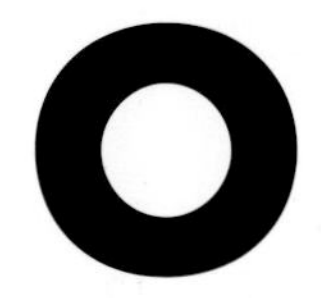

Astrid Stavro's
Favorite Futura Letter
Is 'o'.

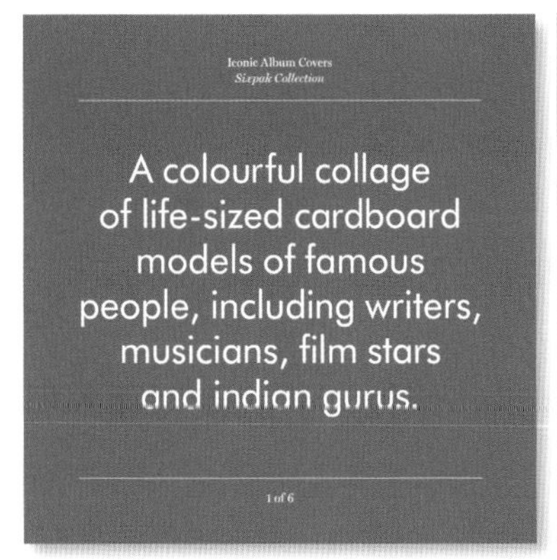

Iconic Album Covers
Sixpak Collection

Illustration of a prism on a black backround refracting white light into the visual spectrum.

2 of 6

Iconic Album Covers
Sixpak Collection

Image of a banana printed on a sticker that peels-off to reveal a flesh-coloured banana underneath.

3 of 6

Iconic Album Covers
Sixpak Collection

A waist-down frontal black and white shot of a male figure in tight jeans, complete with a working zipper.

4 of 6

Iconic Album Covers
Sixpak Collection

Diagram of an image representing the white radio waveforms of pulsar CP 1919 on a black background.

5 of 6

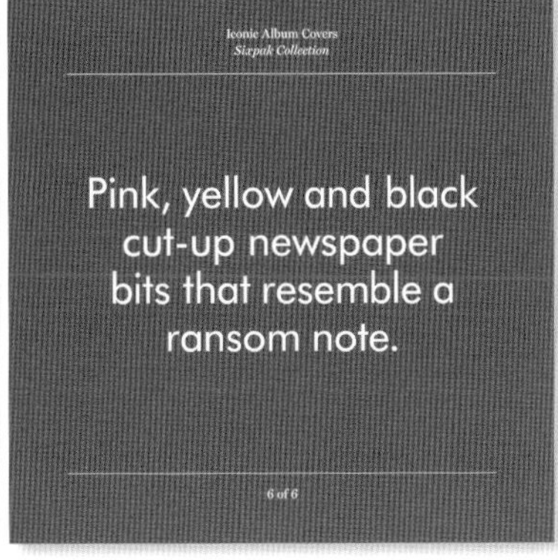

01	02
03	04
05	06

Typeface In Use
Futura Medium

01
Sgt. Pepper's Lonely Hearts Club Band
The Beatles
Designed by Peter Blake

02
Dark Side of the Moon
Pink Floyd
Designed by Hipgnosis
Illustration by George Hardie

03
The Velvet Underground & Nico
The Velvet Underground
Designed by Andy Warhol

04
Sticky Fingers
The Rolling Stones
Designed by Craig Braun
Conceived by Andy Warhol

05
Unknown Pleasures
Joy Division
Designed by Peter Saville

06
Nevermind the Bollocks
The Sex Pistols
Designed by Jamie Reid

www.
thisisgaf.
com

éditeur d'objets
et surfaces

gaf®

Objets :
Nappes
Toiles cirées
Voilages et stores
Parasols
Surfaces :
Sol pvc (dalles)
Carrelage
Papier peint
Plateaux

gaf

ABCDEFGHIJK
LMNOPQRSTUVWXYZ
0123456789,+=/:?
abcdefghijk
lmnopqrstuvwxyz

In our
stuff
we
trust

Gaf Brand Identity
2010 – Corporate identity
Client Gaf éditions
Design TRAFIK (Pierre Rodière)

Creation of the Gaf visual identity decoration brand. Creation of the logotype and its declinations—print, packaging, website.

Typeface In Use
CG Futura

TRAFIK's Favorite
Futura Letter Is 'i'.

"For its really compact and dense look."

www.
thisisgaf.
com
Nappe : bonjour
Design : Trafik
Nappe : Hamburger
Design : Fanette Mellier
Nappe : Hamburger
Design : Fanette Mellier
FAIRE
CUIRE
UN

Much Love From #2
2009 – Poster
Client Mascotte Club, Zurich
Design Jonas Hegi

Poster for a party series at Zurich Mascotte. Kinky bands and DJs together at one night. The poster should look different than normal concert posters—it's a poster not everyone likes. A special edition of the poster – as you can see – was manually silk-screened with different colors by Lisa Mettier.

i

Jonas Hegi's Favorite Futura Letter Is 'i'.

"I was looking for geometrical sans with condensed styles. Futura with its nice condensed style fitted perfectly with the illustration."

Typeface In Use
Futura, Helvetica,
Avant Garde,
Hoefler Text

"To underline the variety of the line-up and to evolve a slightly retro character."

Makoto
2008 – Poster
Client Zerwirk Club
Design C100 Purple Haze (Clemens Baldermann)

Promotional materials for a nightclub.

C100 Purple Haze's
Favorite Futura Letter
Is 'e'.

SELEKTA!
SELEKTA!
SELEKTA!
Makoto
Human Elements / Good Looking / Hospital / Innerground — Tokyo
Deeizm
Human Elements / Good Looking / Liquid V / Bingo / Valve — London
Tobestar + Ryan
Southern Sessions — Munich / Frankfurt
FR / 02 / 05 / 08
ZERWIRK
Ledererstrasse 3 / 80331 München — Doors open: 23.00 PM
dance different
HUMAN ELEMENTS
DEEIZM

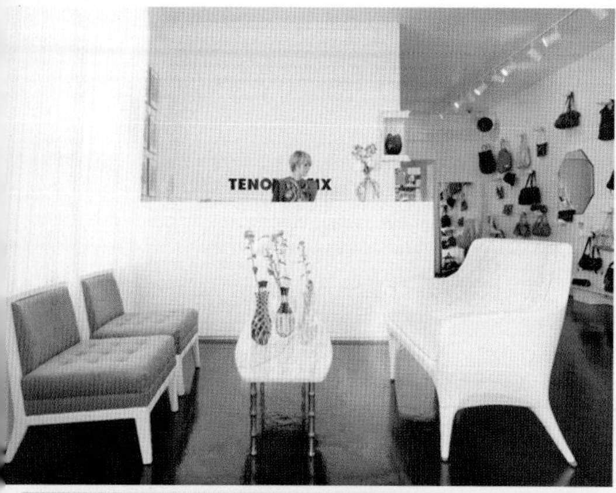

TenOverSix
2009 – Brand identity
Client TenOverSix
Design Roanne Adams, Cynthia Ratsabouth, Zack Nathanson

TenOverSix, boutique and gallery-like installation space in Los Angeles offers high-concept designer accessories. Ingeniously derived from the owner, Kristen Lee's fascination with the book *Alice in Wonderland*—we named and branded the boutique after the "10/6" (or ten pounds six pence) read on Mad Hatter's hat. We explored the object of contemporary price tags, borrowed our color palette from monopoly money, and played with scale as a nod to the whimsy.

Typeface In Use
Futura Extra Black BT, Times New Roman, Firenze

Roanne Adams' Favorite Futura Letter Is 'X'.

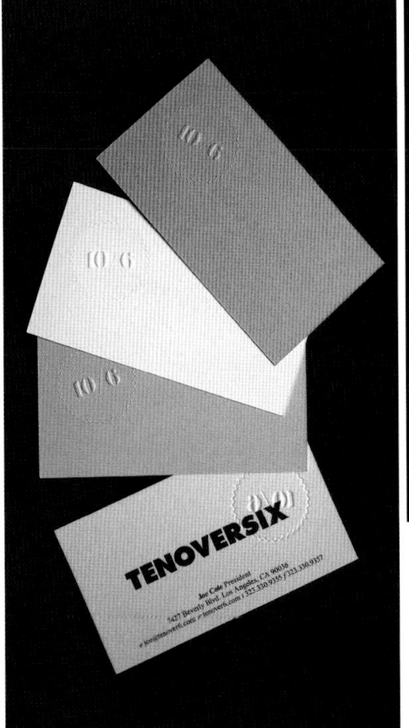

"Futura Extra Black BT was chosen for its boldness, and Firenze because of its similar appearance to Bodoni which is used a lot with fashion."

Typeface In Use
Futura Extra Bold

"A bold and screaming typeface was needed to create this statement."

Gewoon Hard Knallen (Just Play Hard)
2009 – Installation, printed self-promotion
Client Self-initiated/commissioned by TENT. Rotterdam 2009
Design/Photography StudioSpass

Gewoon Hard Knallen (Just Play Hard) is a provocative reference to the vision of one of Rotterdam's former leading design studios. While "hard work" was the designer's maxim in the 1980s, for this generation it's about making a noise. *Gewoon Hard Knallen* is an an-amorphous mural; it plays with the laws of perspective and is only fully visible and readable from one set position. The card consists out of three pieces. One largely-cut card depicting a photo taken onsite, of the installation itself, and two personalized business cards placed on top of the larger photo card. For this project two similar photos were taken of the installation. For this project, two similar photos were taken in total – one was of the installation itself and another with designers of StudioSpass in the installation. The two business cards are smaller cut-outs of two individual members of StudioSpass standing in the actual setting with intallation as the background. These smaller cards are then placed over the original installation photo, to create the scene of two graphic designers residing in their work, with a full print background, create by the larger photo card. When the business cards are removed, the photos of the StudioSpass designers are literally taken with you, revealing a bare and designer-less installation photo. Upon "taking the designers with you" you also receive all necessary contact information you might need, and find it hidden neatly on the back of the business card. In this way StudioSpass not only offers insight into some of their more prominent and personal work and work ethic, though an original and eye catching campaign, but also allows the viewer to become immediately familiar with the designers, their style and way of working.

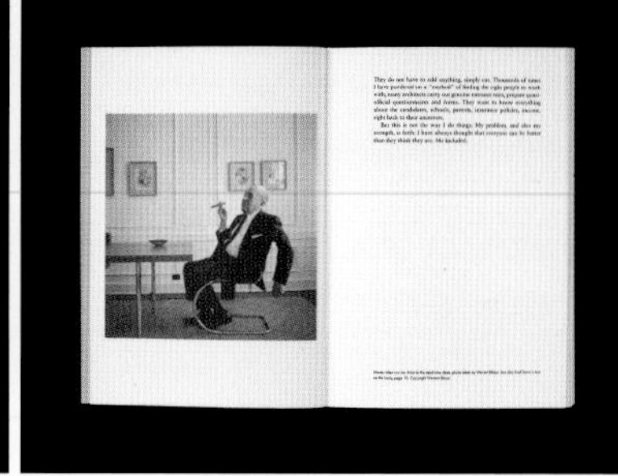

Crucial Words
Conditions for Contemporary Architecture
2008 – Book
Client Birkhäuser Verlag, Switzerland
Design Henrik Nygren Design, Sweden

Typeface In Use
Futura EF

A book, based on 31 words, which proves that architecture is everything from *Architects* to *Why*.

"Is there a better typeface for a book on architecture than Futura?"

Typeface In Use
Futura EF

"Is there a better typeface for a book on architecture and design than Futura?"

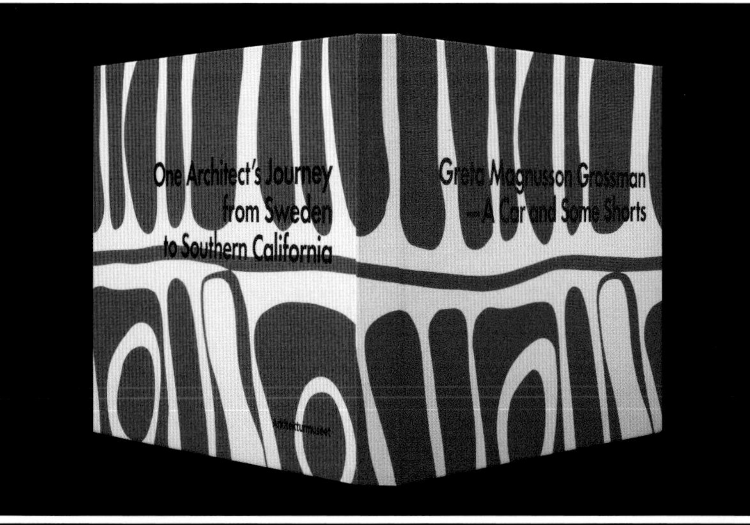

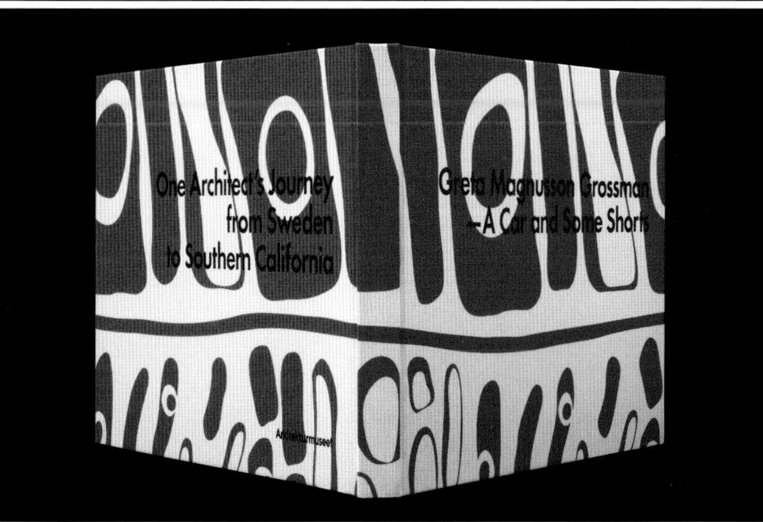

Greta Magnusson Grossman
– A Car and Some Shorts. One Architect's Journey from Sweden to Soutern California
2010 – Book, exhibition
Client The Swedish Museum of Architecture, Sweden
Design Henrik Nygren Design, Sweden

Book and exhibition identity corresponding to Greta Magnusson Grossman's words "The easiest way to show what you can do is to do it on your own".

Typeface In Use
Futura EF

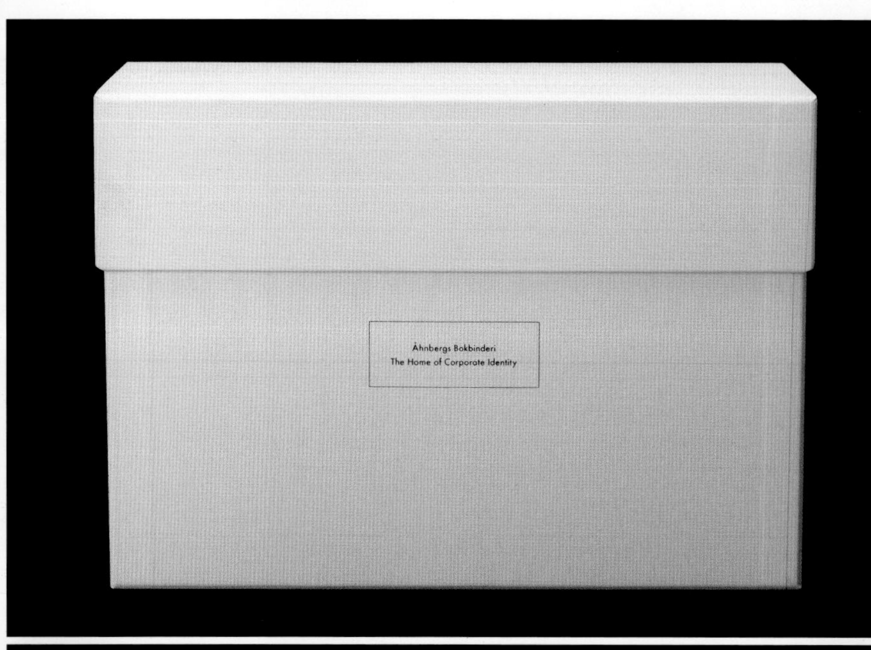

Åhnbergs Bokbinderi, The Home of Corporate Identity
2009 – Packaging
Client Åhnbergs Bokbinderi (Åhnberg's Bookbinders, Sweden)
Design Henrik Nygren Design, Sweden

The 12 most common projects that this bookbinder is producing on a daily basis. All in the same standard size. All dressed in white. All for the imagination.

"Is there a better typeface for a bookbinder than Futura?"

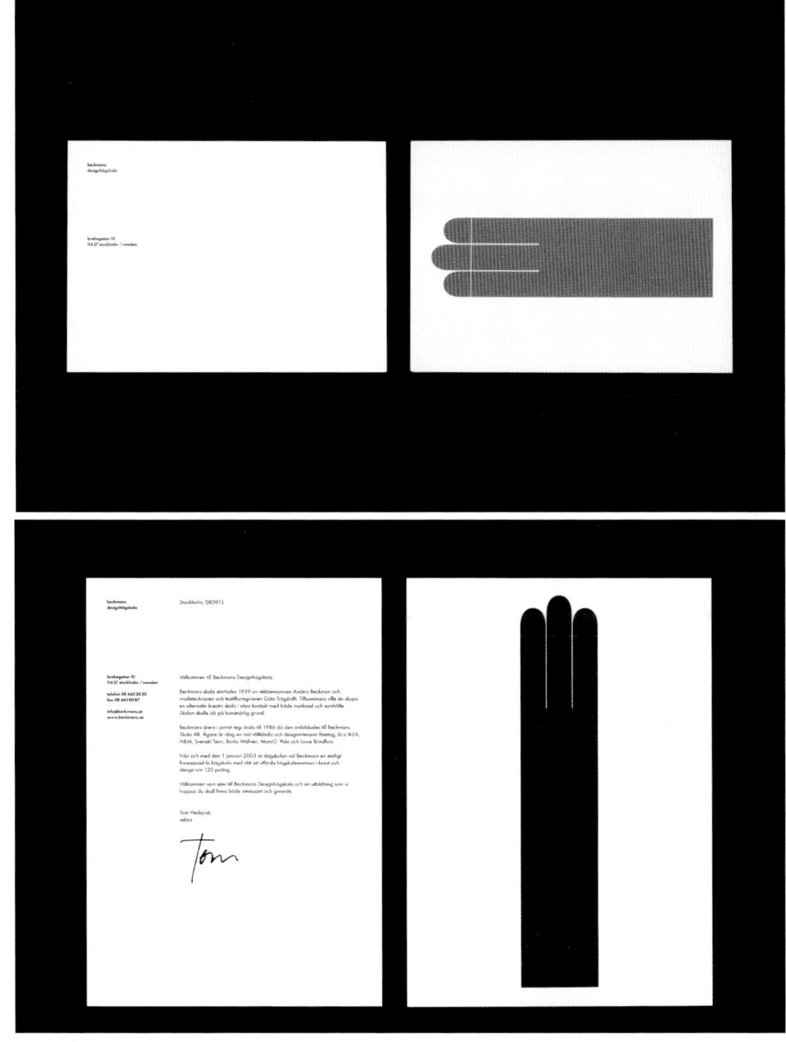

Beckmans College of Design
2009 – Graphic identity
Client Beckmans College of Design, Sweden
Design Henrik Nygren Design, Sweden

Sweden's leading design college since 1939. An identity for the college and their three departments – Visual Communication, Fashion and Product Design.

Typeface In Use
Futura EF

"Is there a better typeface for a design college than Futura?"

beckmans
college of design

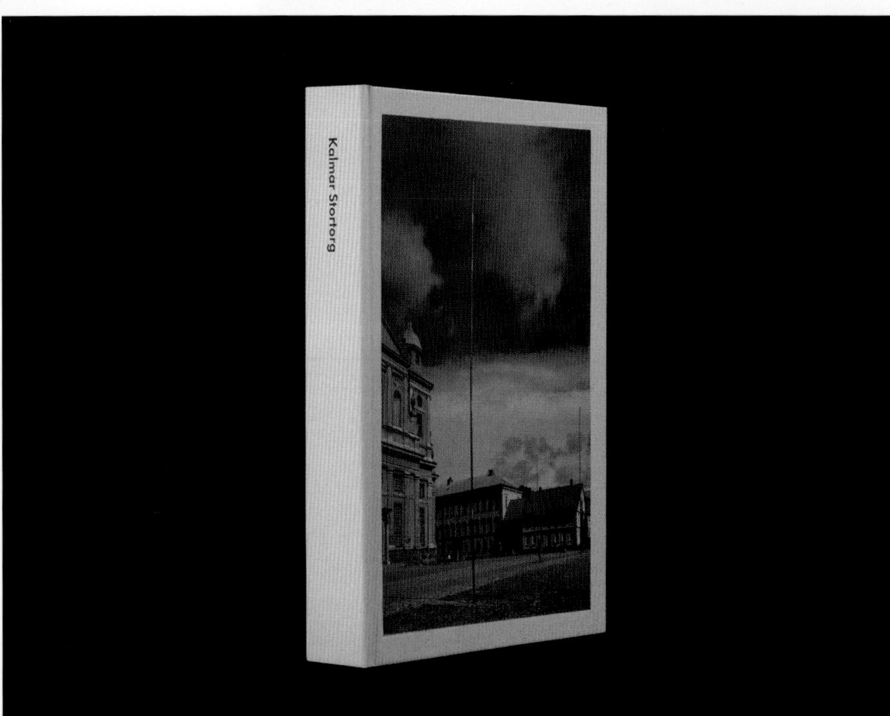

Typeface In Use
Futura EF

"Is there a better type-face for a book on art and archi-tecture than Futura?"

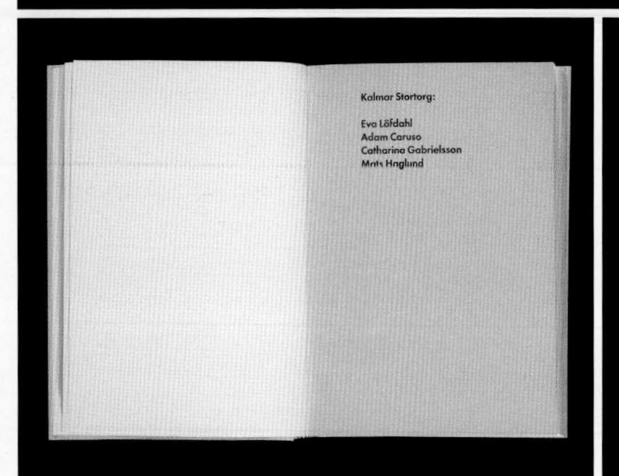

Kalmar Grand Square:
Art/Architecture in Urban Space
2008 – Book
Client The National Public Art Council Sweden
Design Henrik Nygren Design, Sweden

Pink uncoated paper. Glossy tritone images. Headlines in Futura. A good old simple recipe.

Typeface In Use
Futura EF

"Is there a better typeface for a king than Futura?"

King Carl XVI Gustaf, 60 years
2008 – Stamp
Client The Royal Swedish Mail, Sweden
Design Henrik Nygren Design, Sweden

You cannot shorten the King's name! You can not crop the King's head! There was a lot of "cannots", in the beginning (and end) of this little (and large) project.

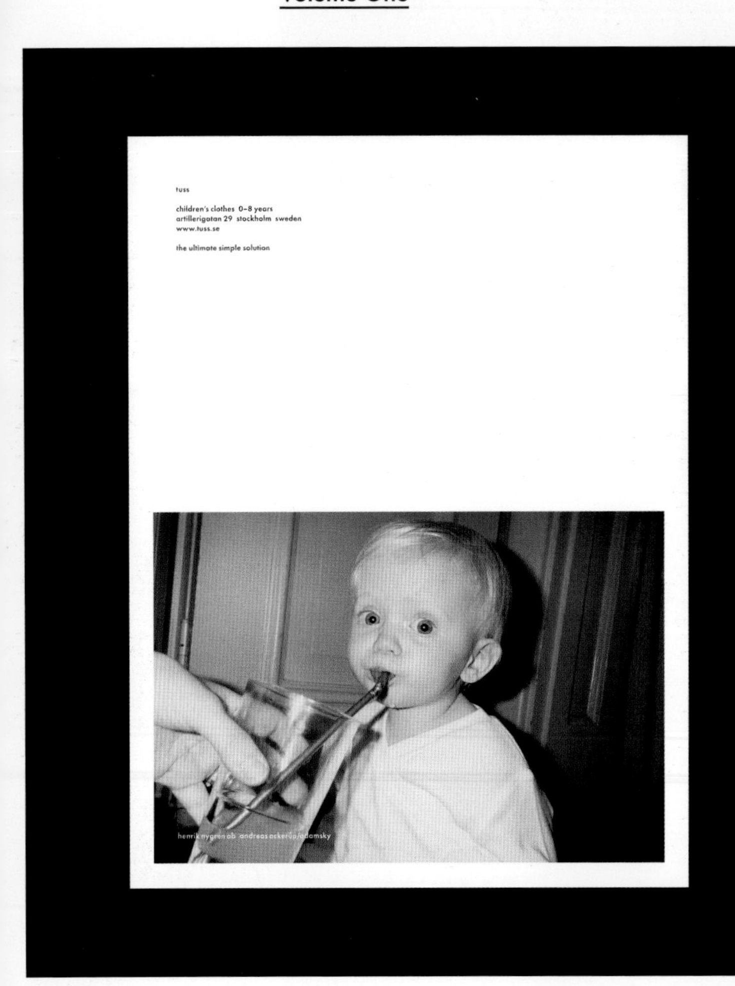

Tuss, The Ultimate Simple Solution
2008 – Graphic identity

Client Tuss, The Ultimate Simple Solution, Sweden
Design Henrik Nygren Design, Sweden

Throughout the whole identity, only one (small) size of lower case letter is used. From labels in cloths to advertising in magazines.

"Is there a better typeface for a children's clothing store than Futura?"

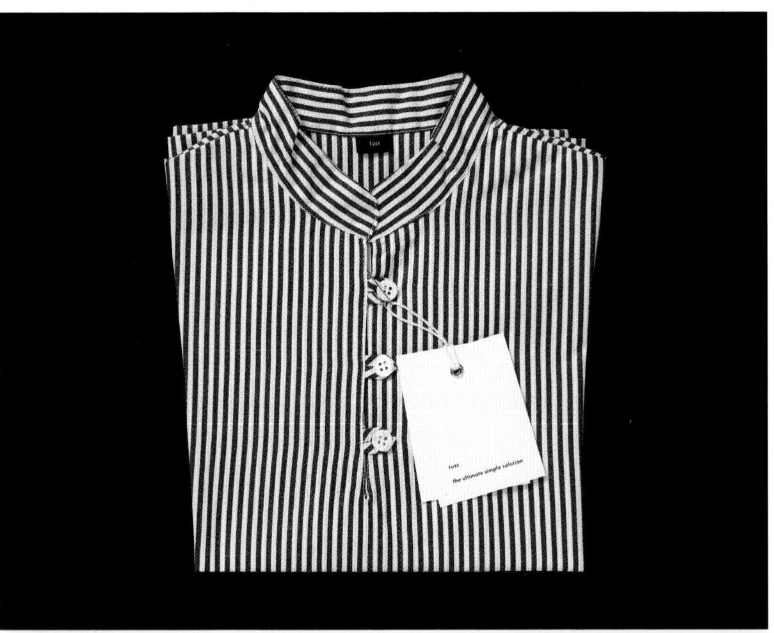

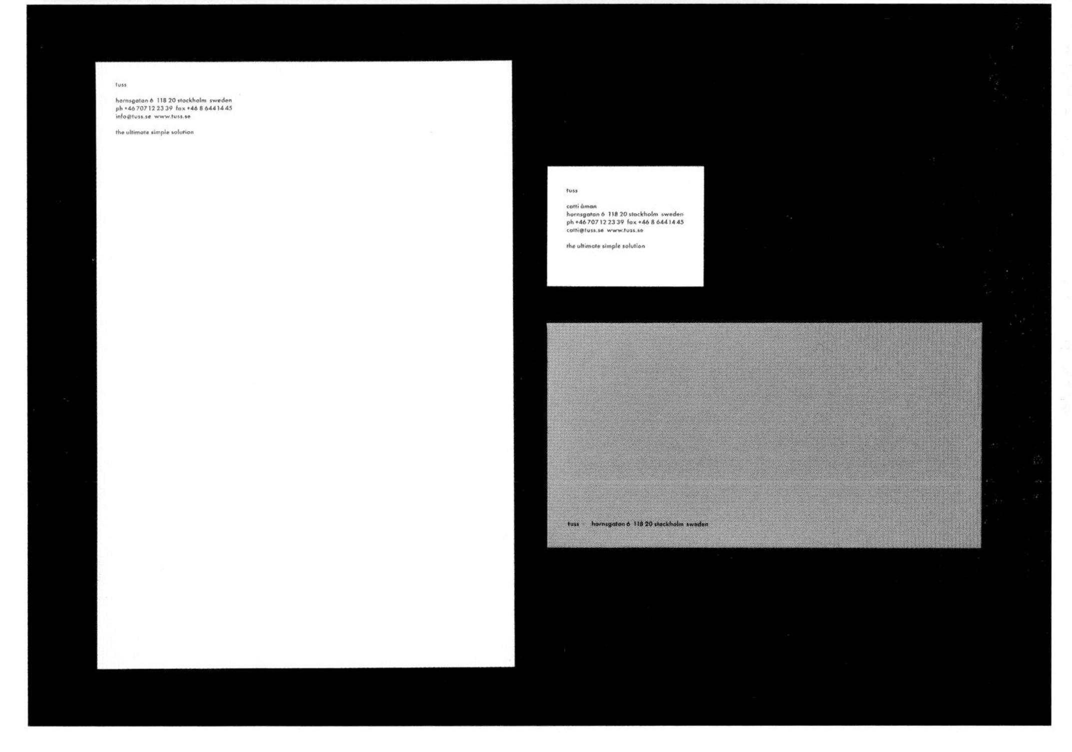

Typeface In Use
Futura EF

Sotbrand (Soot fire)
2008 – Book
Client Modernista Publishers, Sweden
Design Henrik Nygren Design, Sweden

A novel about an artist's life, an accident, a turn in this person's life. Printed on the whitest possible cloth and whitest possible paper in the darkest possible way.

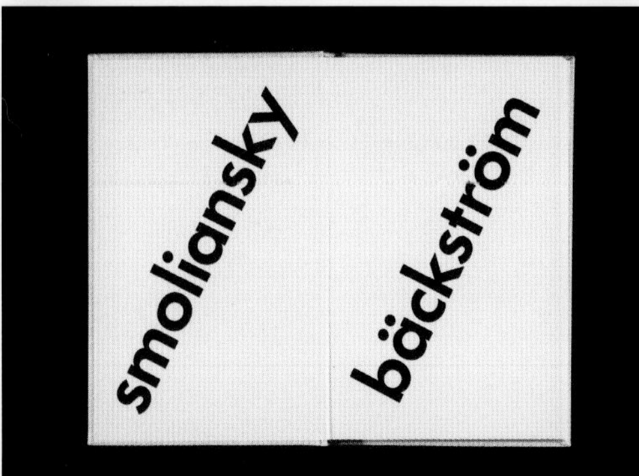

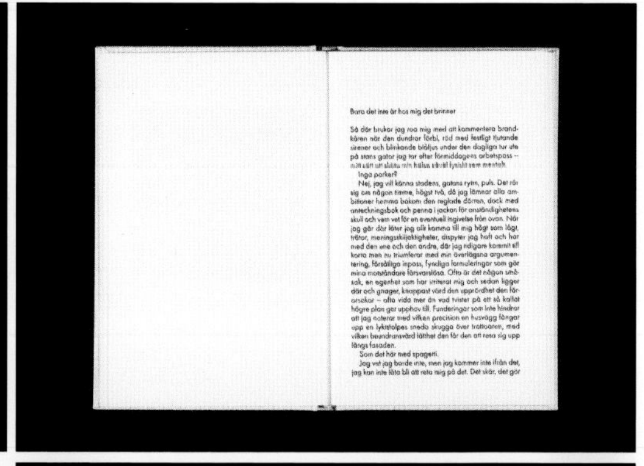

Bara det inte är hos mig det brinner

Så där brukar jag roa mig med att kommentera brandkåren när den dundrar förbi, röd med festligt tjutande sirener och blinkande blåljus under den dagliga tur ute på stans gator jag tar efter förmiddagens arbetspass – mitt sätt att sköta min hälsa såväl fysiskt som mentalt.

Inga parker?

Nej, jag vill känna stadens, gatans rytm, puls. Det rör sig om någon timme, högst två, då jag lämnar alla ambitioner hemma bakom den reglade dörren, dock med anteckningsbok och penna i jackan för anständighetens skull och vem vet för en eventuell ingivelse från ovan. När jag går där låter jag allt komma till mig högt som lågt, trätor, meningsskiljaktigheter, dispyter jag haft och har med den ene och den andre, där jag tidigare kommit till korta men nu triumferar med min överlägsna argumentering, försåtliga inpass, fyndiga formuleringar som gör mina motståndare försvarslösa. Ofta är det någon småsak, en egenhet som har irriterat mig och sedan ligger där och gnager, knappast värd den upprördhet den förorsakar – ofta vida mer än vad tvister på ett så kallat högre plan ger upphov till. Funderingar som inte hindrar att jag noterar med vilken precision en husvägg fångar upp en lyktstolpes sneda skugga över trottoaren, med vilken beundransvärd lätthet den får den att resa sig upp längs fasaden.

Som det här med spagetti.

Jag vet jag borde inte, men jag kommer inte ifrån det, jag kan inte låta bli att reta mig på det. Det skär, det gör

Typeface In Use
Futura EF

"Is there a better typeface for a novel than Futura?"

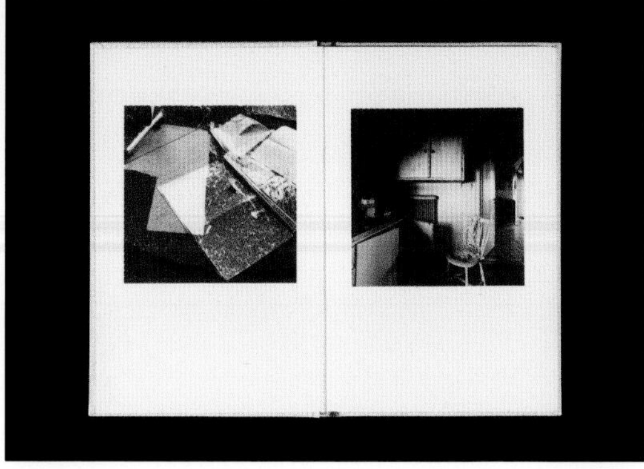

"Is there a better typeface for a book on photography than Futura?"

Gunnar Smoliansky,
One Picture at a Time
2009 – Book
Client GUN, Germany (Steidl Verlag)
Design Henrik Nygren Design, Sweden

A book on one of Sweden's most important photographer's work, between 1952 and 2008. All 285 images in the book are the vintage prints, shown in full scale. On the other hand, all the types are shown in only two sizes.

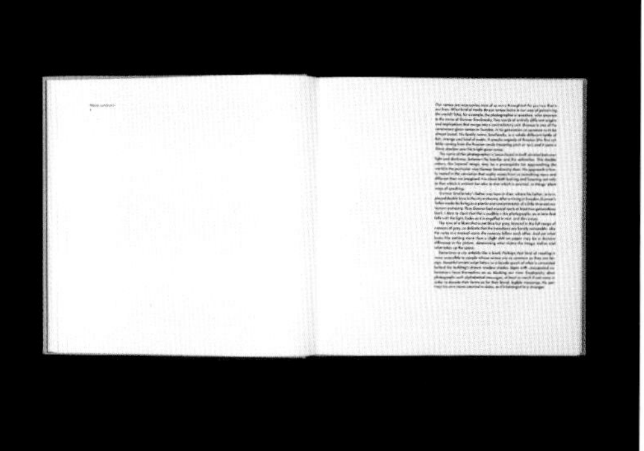

E

Bendita Gloria & Dani Navarro's Favorite Futura Letter Is 'E'.

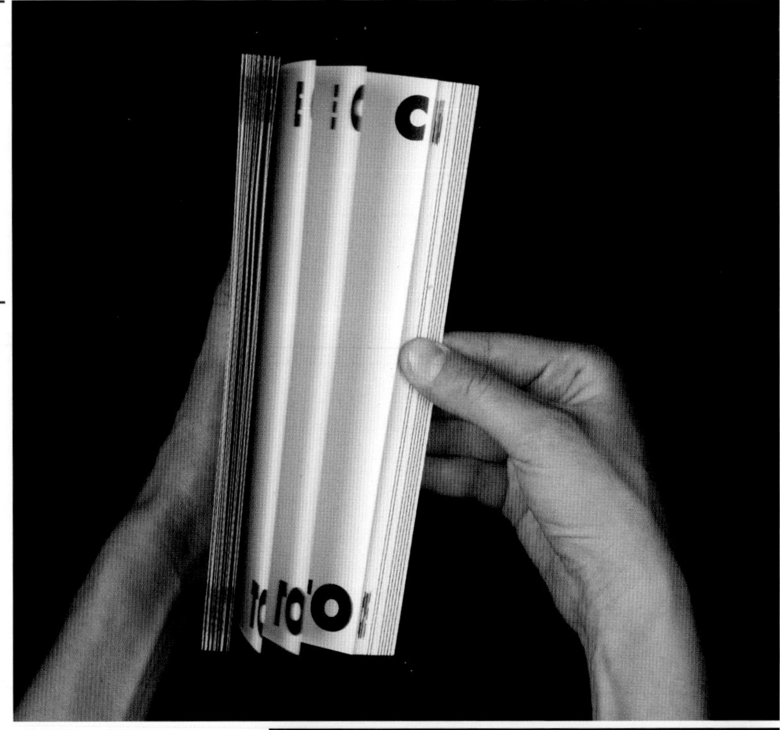

"It's big and bold, it's a good font to talk about entertainment."

Typeface In Use
Futura Extra Bold, Utopia

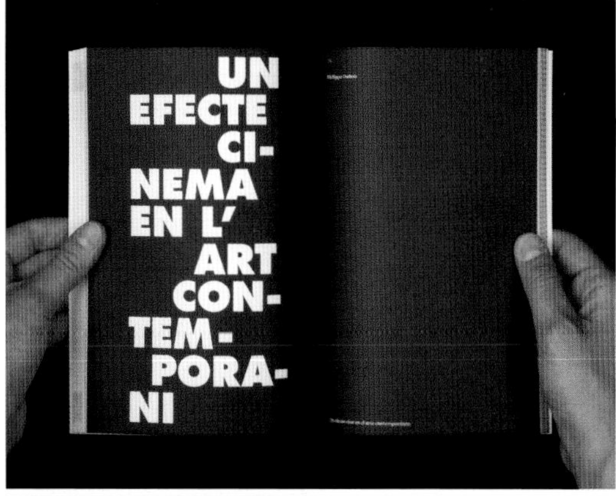

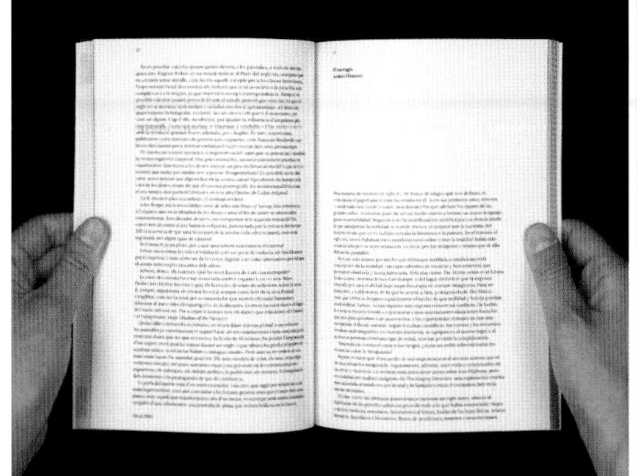

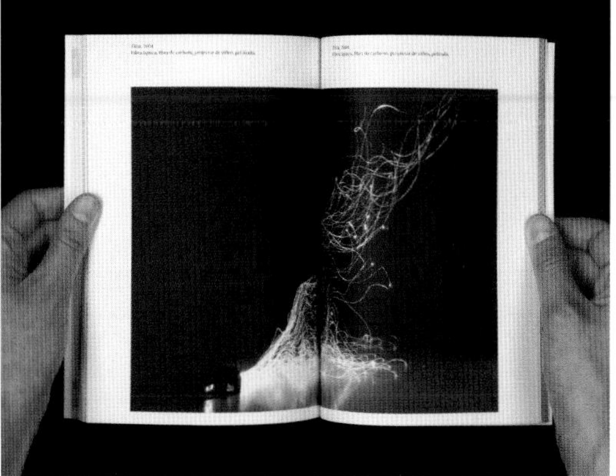

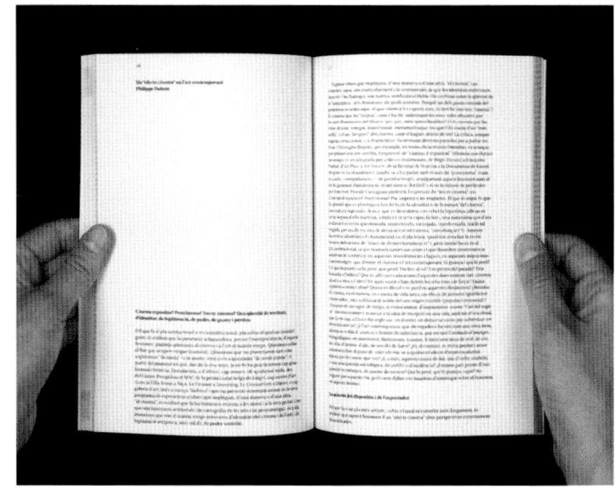

Efecte cinema
2009 – Catalog
Client Joana Hurtado, Eloi Grasset
Design Dani Navarro, Bendita Gloria

The *Efecte Cinema* exhibition offers an insight into the influence played by films in art. The catalog begins with a flipbook as a kind of opening title sequence.

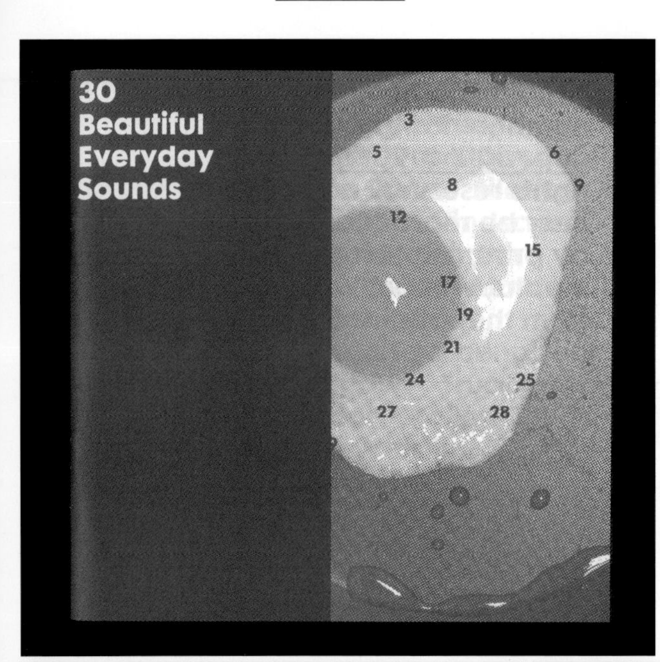

30 Beautiful Everyday Sounds
2009 – Book
Client KIDP
Design Why Not Smile
(Hoon Kim)

This collection of bold, black and white pixelated patterns was created using a system that translates sound into pattern, relying on pitch and volume to determine the size and shape of the pixels. Graphic designer interprets 30 sounds, ranging from a baby's sneeze and a ticking alarm clock to the sound of bread being sliced, or of silence.

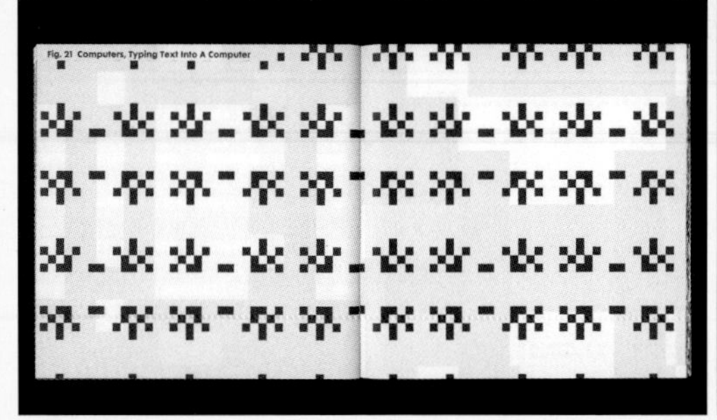

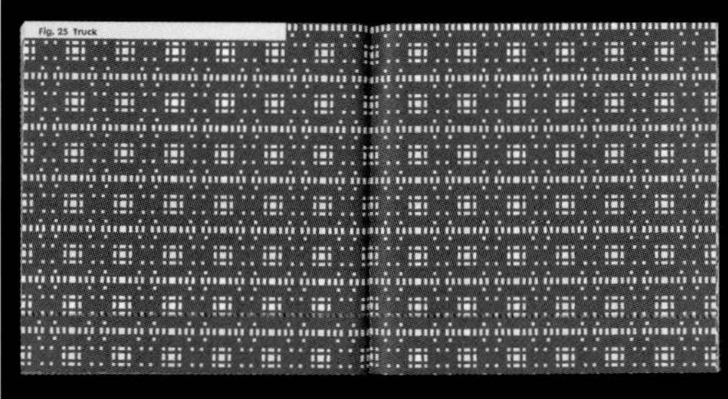

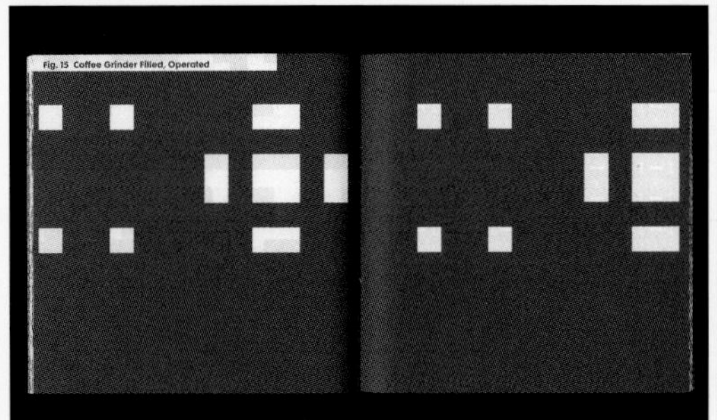

Alarm Clock[1] Automatic Washing Machine[2] Baby Crying[3] Baby Sneezing[4] Footsteps[5] Front Door[6] Frying An Egg[7] Gas Stove[8] Silence[9] Bath[10] Bicycle[11] Bread[12] Windscreen Wipers[13] Horn[14] Coffee Grinder[15] Kettle[16] Microwave Oven[17] Motor Cycle[18] Printing Machinery[19] Refrigerator[20] Computer[21] Brick Wall[22] Mug[23] Window[24] Truck[25] Electric Drill[26] Teapot[27] Toilet[28] Vacuum Cleaner[29] Whistling Kettle[30]

Typeface In Use
Futura Maxi

"Geometric aspects of Futura explain a concept of the project: one basic unit increases."

Oscar Properties

Oscar Properties
2008 – Corporate Identity
Client Oscar Properties
Design Acne Art Department (Daniel Carlsten)

Visual identity and stationery for a real estate company that successfully manages to marry architectural influences from Swedish modernism with an ambience of New York lofts.

Typeface In Use
Renner Bold

"Futura was one of the most popular typefaces of the Swedish Modern era. Oscar Properties deals with a lot of houses from that era."

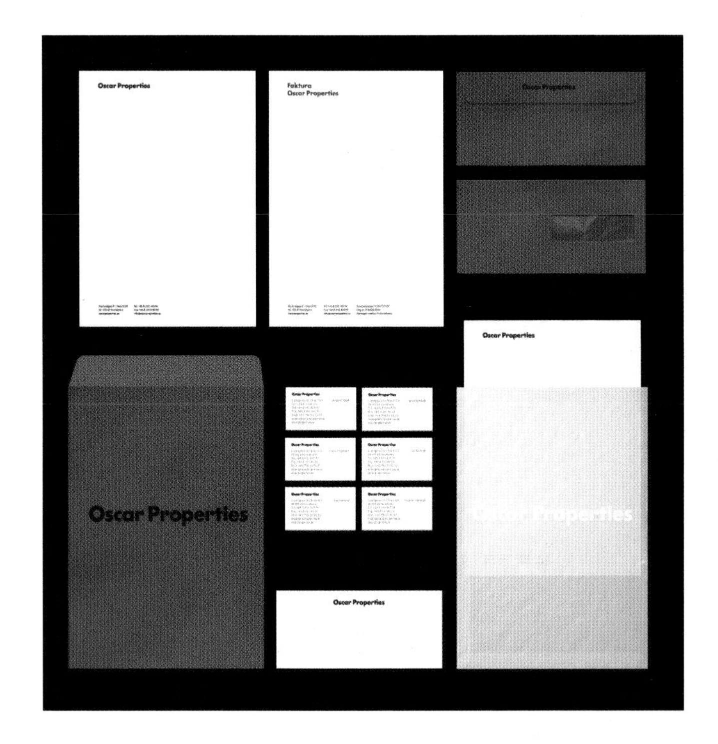

Daniel Carlsten's Favorite Futura Letter Is 'r'.

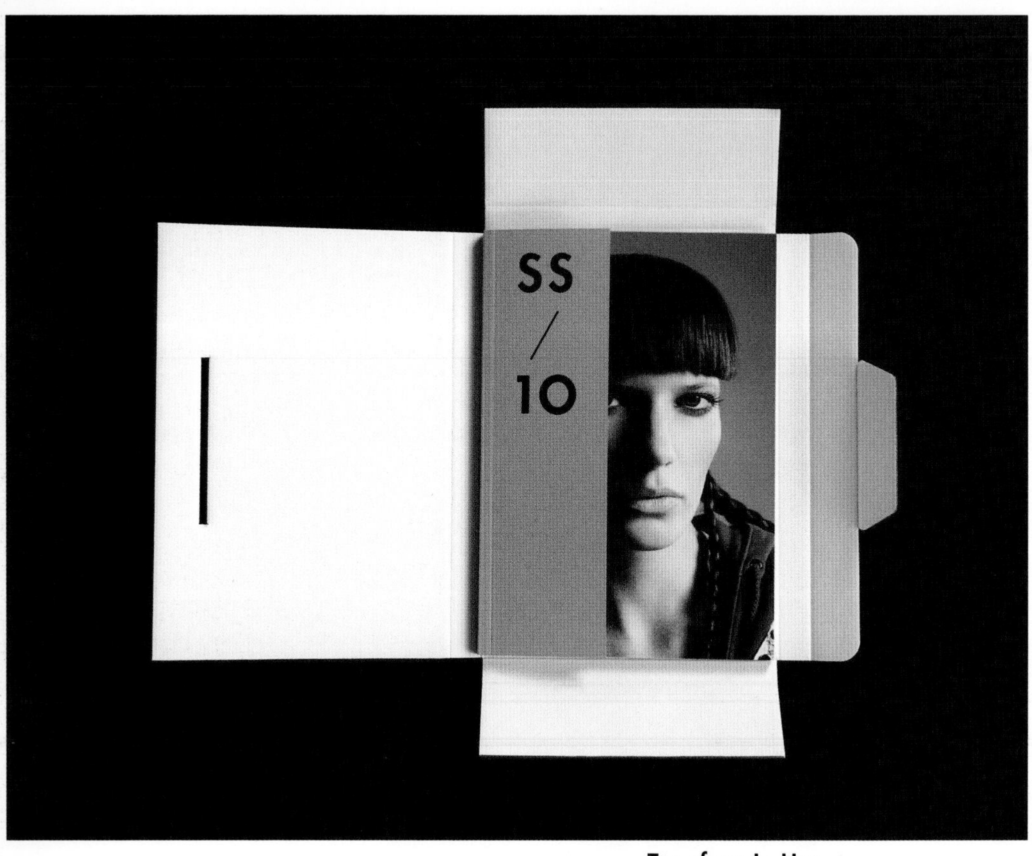

Typeface In Use
Futura

Topshop SS '10 Lookbook
2010 – Packaging, book
Client Topshop
Design Shaz Madani

Packaging and catalog design for Topshop's main line Spring/Summer 2010 lookbook.

Shaz Madani's
Favorite Futura Letter
Is 'M'.

Featuring:
Six DJ's (House & RnB)
Mixing live with instrumental artists
& Live video show
Saturday 14th February
At Posthallen Arena
Adr: Prinsensgate 8, Oslo
Doors open: 21.00
Ticket sales & information
Call: +47 936 87 492
Email: post@ofwparty.com
Online sales: www.ofwparty.com
Website login VIP CODE: OFW
At the door: 350 Kr.
Pre sales: 250 Kr.
AFTER
PARTY

OSLO
FASHION
WEEK

OSLO
FASHION
WEEK
POSTHALLEN
PARTY

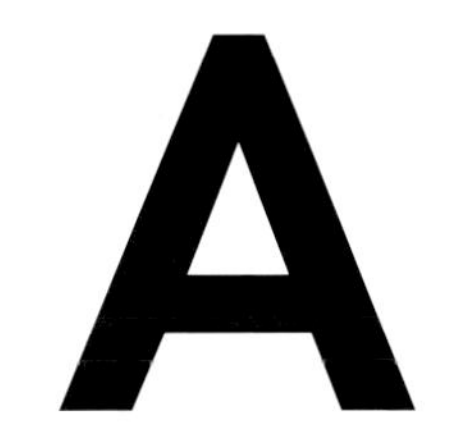

Robin Snasen Rengård's Favorite Futura Letter Is 'A'.

"It's just epic in the way it reaches for the sky."

Typeface In Use
Futura, Bodoni & bespoke typeface

"Futura and Bodoni have a long history in the world of fashion and it felt natural to choose this as the main typeface. The identity changes each year except the main typeface, Futura, so it had to be a classic."

Oslo Fashion Week
2009 – Identity
Client Oslo Fashion Week
Design Robin Snasen Rengård
Photography Joakim Gomnes, Joachim Norvik, Lars Petter Pettersen, Einar Aslaksen, Det tredje Oyet, Gil Inoue, Dusan Reljin, Robin Snasen Rengård, Nick McLean

I wanted to use the main tools a fashion designer works with, namely fabric, and interpret this as a graphic designer.

R

us' Favorite Futura Letter Is 'R'.

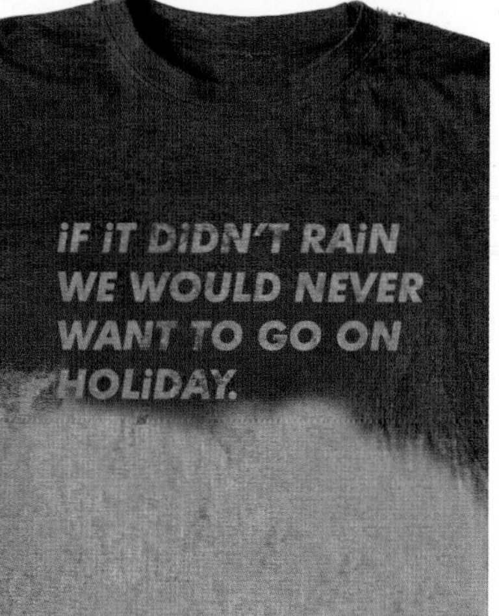

Typeface In Use
Futura Bold Italic

Rain Positive
2008 – T-shirts, posters
Design us (design studio)

T-shirts and posters were produced to persuade people to look at the rain in a different way. Through a unique printing process the T-shirts and posters only reveal their message when exposed to the rain.

Typeface In Use
Futura Bold Italic

"Its presence; also it was the only typeface that maintained its shape in lowercase. I also knew it would work wonderfully in italic."

R

Sort Design's Favorite Futura Letter Is 'R'.

Todd Architects Promotional Materials
2009 – Corporate promotional materials
Client Todd Architects
Design Sort Design

Having worked with Todd Architects for a number of years, and after implementing a full redesign of their corporate identity, Sort were commissioned to develop promotional materials to showcase the practice's recent work. The final pack included a presentation box, a portfolio booklet and inserts highlighting the practice's work in various sectors. The print featured gold and transparent pearlescent foil-blocked finishes on uncoated and glossy stock.

Typeface In Use
Futura Bold

"The Modernist clarity of the typeface reflects the architectural aims of the client's practice."

TODD

BUILDING
FOR THE
FUTURE WITH
TODD
ARCHITECTS

TODD
TODD

Typeface In Use
Futura Book

"Futura is one of the corporate typefaces of Asos."

5

Gloor & Jandl's Favorite Futura Number Is '5'.

Asos Lookbooks
2009 – Book design
Client Kilimanjaro Art & Design, London, UK
Design Gloor & Jandl, Kilimanjaro Art & Design, London, UK

Lookbooks A/W 2009 and S/S 2010 for the London based fashion retailer Asos. Womenswear and menswear is divided in two similar editions. They appear with a thread stitching, varying papers and formats.

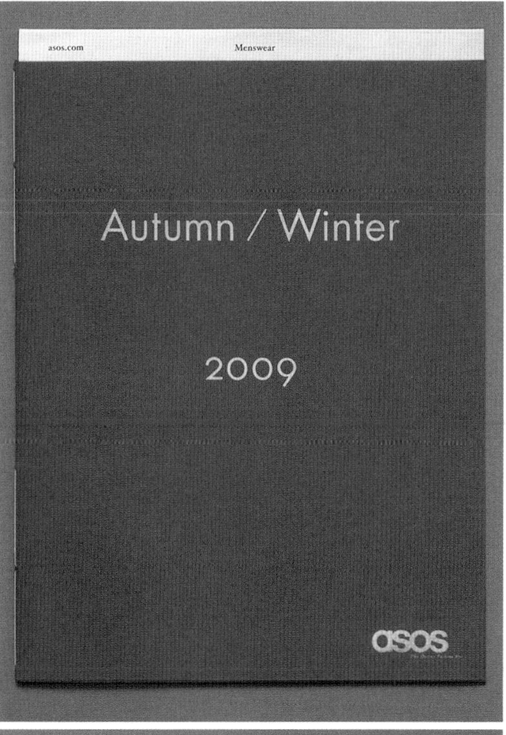

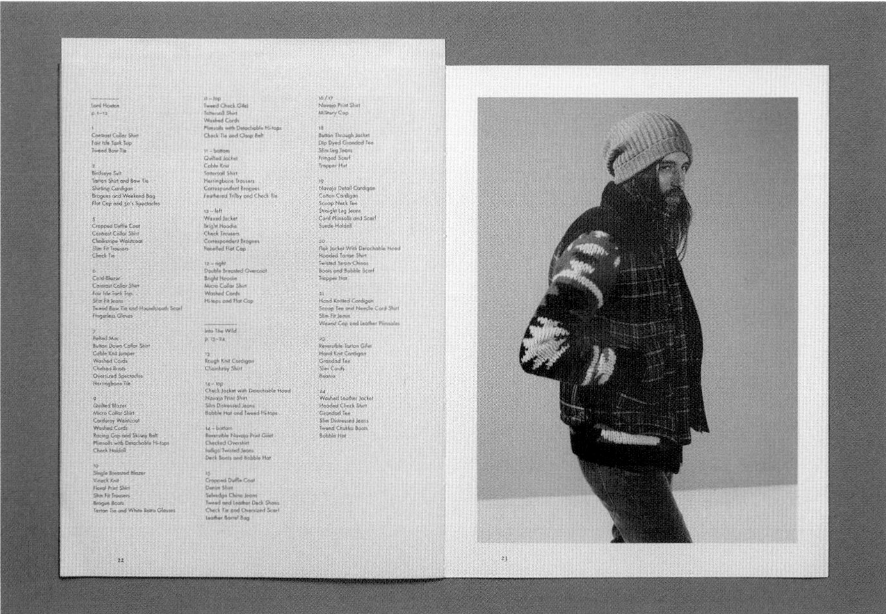

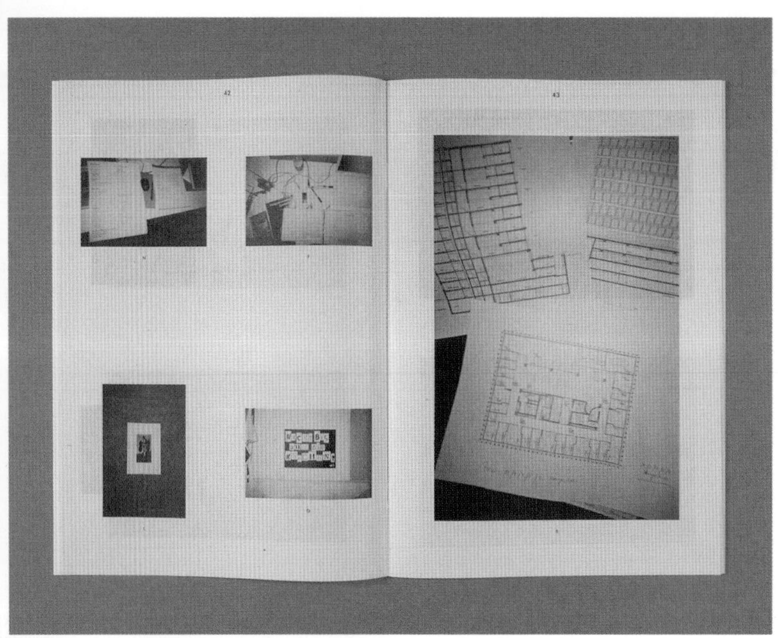

Typeface In Use
Futura BT Medium

Diploma Catalog 2008
2008 – Book design
Client Zurich University of the Arts, Graduates, Zurich, CH
Design Gloor & Jandl

Publication about the diploma projects by visual communication graduates of Zurich University of the Arts. Due to the fact that the works were not finished by the time the catalog was produced, a disposable camera was given to every graduate, to document their working procedure during the four months of their projects.

Projektbeschrieba /
Biografien

A
Marcel Bomert
Über den Tellerrand

B
Marie Bär
Zu Recht finden

C
Celine Beyeler / Andrea Koch
Kristalloid

D
Andrea Bissig / Ira Giesen
no excuse!

Typeface In Use
Futura Std, Bold & Medium

"Legibility"

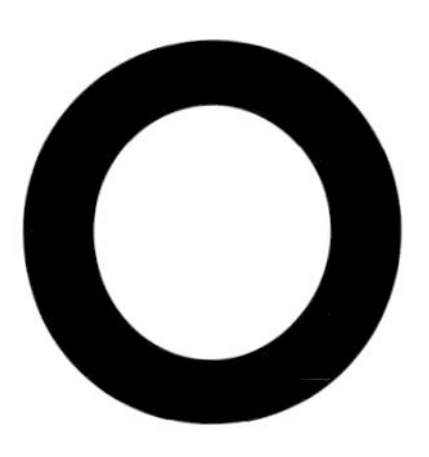

Joe Hinder's Favorite Futura Letter Is 'O'.

Bath Spa Degree Show 2009
2009 – Poster, signage
Client Bath Spa University
Design Joe Hinder
Photography Jack Williams
Signage Joe Hinder, Stephanie Ireland

Designed for Bath School of Art and Design Degree Show 2009. Litho printed on recycled stock. The poster becomes an invite when folded.

Ongoing
2010 – Poster
Client Graphic Design Festival
Breda, the Netherlands
Design Pot & van der Velden

Every two years in Breda, the Netherlands, there is the Graphic Design Festival. For the festival we were asked to design a poster in response to a manifesto by Bruce Mau. Our starting point for the poster was Rule 43 of this manifesto *Listen Carefully*, and we translated it into "How to listen carefully in ten steps". Forty-three designers were asked by design collective GDV, the curator of the festival, to interpret 43 statements in 43 posters with the theme "Ongoing, an interpretation of Bruce Mau's incomplete manifesto for growth". The poster was exhibited during the festival.

Pot & van der Velden's Favorite Futura Letter Is 'E'.

HOW TO LIS-TEN CARE-FULLY
— LISTEN CAREFULLY —
FROM 'INCOMPLETE MANIFESTO'
BY BRUCE MAU
— ONTWERP —
POT & VAN DER VELDEN
GRAFISCH ONTWERPERS
WWW.POTVANDERVELDEN.NL
I'm the type of person whose mind is racing 24 hours a day. Growing up it was hard for me to pay close attention to things that I weren't that interested in. The positive side of it is that if I'm interested in something I'll focus on it better than anybody else around.
I've conducted over 100 interviews on the radio and on camera with various entertainers and people. So, I had to develop better listening skills. I've used those skills to apply them to personal relationships and everyday life. In this article I'll give you a few steps so you'll learn how to listen more carefully and better to people.
Difficulty: Moderate
Instructions
Things You'll Need:
• Patience
• Understanding
• Better awareness
1. Step 1
In order to listen more carefully to someone, you have to take a deep breath. Calm yourself down.
2. Step 2
Keep great eye contact.
3. Step 3
Pay close attention to what is being said. Block everything else out that's going on around you.
4. Step 4
Remember.. as Abe Lincoln said.. "To ease another's heartache is to forget one's own." - Make it a challenge for yourself to listen to the other person.. challenge yourself to listen closely and make effective responses.
5. Step 5
One way to show you're listening and to make sure you understand what is being said is to repeat the speaker's thoughts in your own words.
that you're engaged in the conversation.. and it's also a great way of helping yourself understand better.
6. Step 6
Don't interrupt! You'll have things that pop into your mind when you're in a conversation... but that doesn't mean you have to blurt them out as soon as you think of them. Hold back... wait until the other person is done and then make your comments.
7. Step 7
Keep an open mind about the subject of the conversation.
Tips & Warnings
It's fine if you think of things to say as the conversation rolls along. Just don't put them out there as soon as you think of something.. find a way to say those things after the person is finished talking.
•
Work on this. Listening is a skill.
•
Don't talk about yourself. It's okay to give examples of something related to the subject that you've experienced. But, remember, it's not always about you. Try to focus more on the person and the subject.
• If none of this works. Then, you're not a good listener. Just pretend you listen to everybody and you'll make it ok in this world.

Colorfull
2008 – Poster
Client Association Destress
Design Neo Neo (Xavier Erni)

Visual communication for a paint jam and concert in Geneva, Switzerland. The idea was to create a *Colorfull* abstract poster. The rectangles represent the different canvases of the paint jam.

Typeface In Use
Futura Medium,
Didot Bold

Têt Cosunam 2010
2010 – Poster, invitation brochure
Client Cosunam, Comité Suisse-Vietnam
Design Neo Neo (Xavier Erni, Thuy-An Hoang)

Visual communication for the Vietnamese new year's eve party in Geneva. The tiger's face is hid den behind the black typography in a white rectangle at the center of the design. The fonts and white surface together form a geometrical pattern that contrasts the tiger's stripes in the background.

Typeface In Use
Futura Medium

Made for Magazine

2009 – Poster
Client Royal Academy of Arts, The Hague, Netherlands
Design Pot & van der Velden
Credits Gerdi Esch, Gwendolyn Keasberry, Hanneke van Leeuwen and Nicky Onderwater

We have printed labels on different color sheets. We used these labels on the poster to announce and promote the launch of the magazine *Made For*.

Typeface In Use
Futura

E

Pot & van der Velden's Favorite Futura Letter Is 'E'.

MADE
FOR
TEXTIEL-
EN MODE-
PUBLICATIE
NU
TE KOOP
MADE
FOR
TEXTIEL-
EN MODE-
PUBLICATIE
NU
TE KOOP
MADE FOR
TEXTIEL-
EN MODE-
MADE
FOR
TEXTIEL-
EN MODE-
PUBLICATIE
NU
TE KOOP

Educate Your Customer 2010 – Poster Design – Kidnap Your Designer (Caroline Dath, Damien Safie & guests)

Cause we're fed
up of being:

lost
phoned for nonsense
surprised at the end of a project
not understood
ambiguous
puppets
pulled back
non communicating
mute
constantly tested
in first line
wankers
only friends
broke
hostages

Typeface In Use
Futura

"Geometric character (and a Futurist idea, in the begining of the 20th century)."

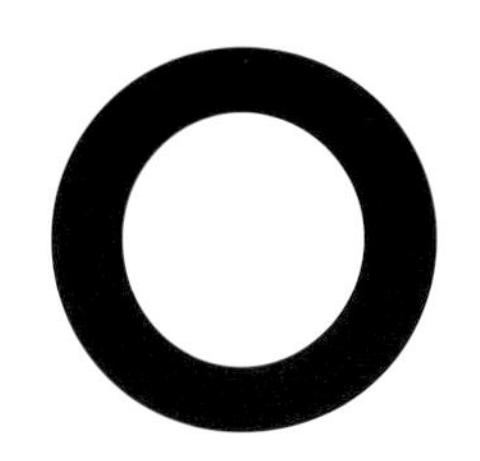

Bisdixit's Favorite Futura Letter Is 'O'.

The Future is Unwritten
2009 – Poster
Design Bisdixit (Pere Alvaro, Àlex Gifreu, Carles Murillo, Sara Santos)

A hopeful sentence in crisis time. The future is unpredictable, unwritten; we present the sentence in a unwritten way, in an in-progress way.

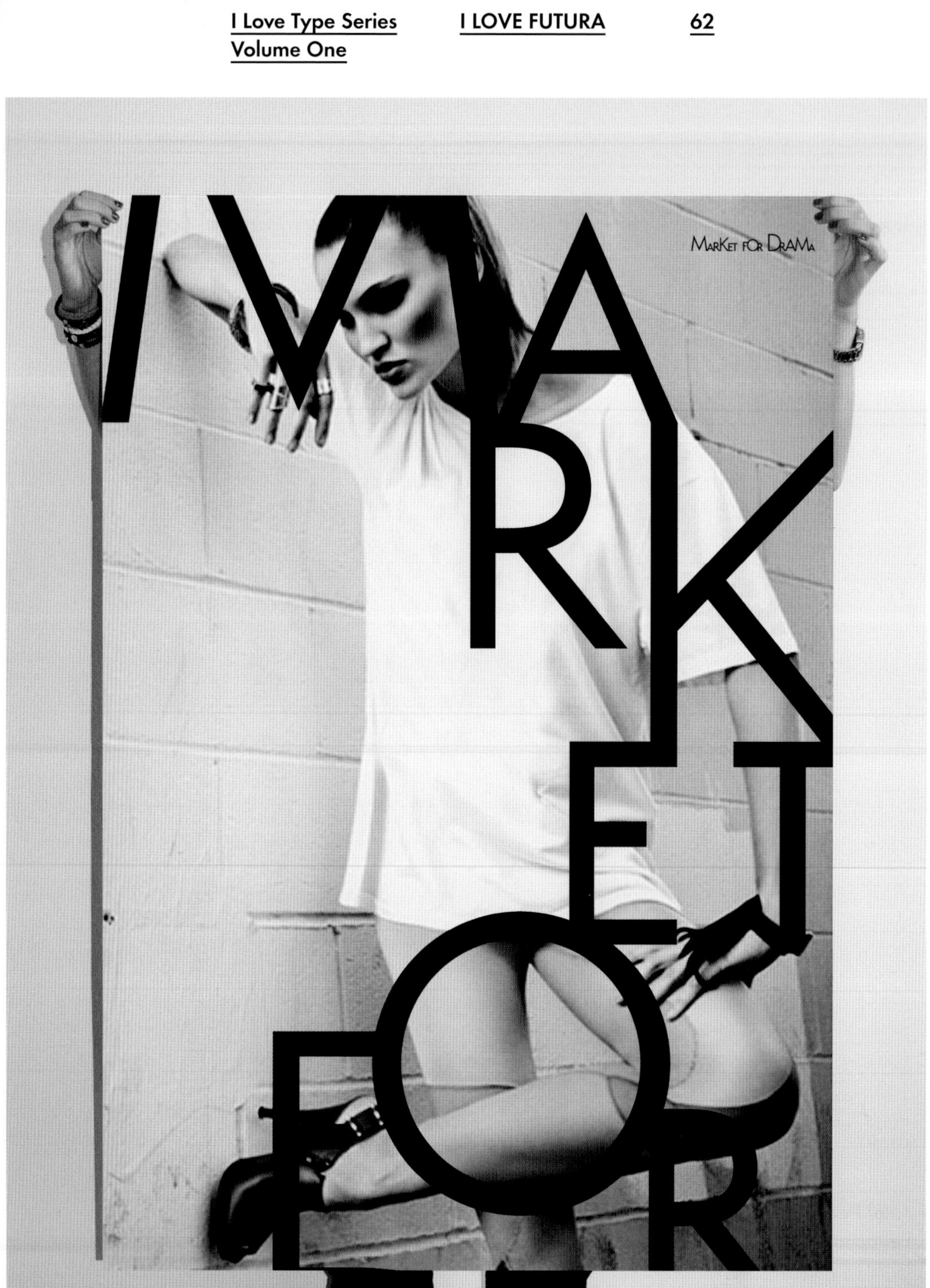
MARKET FOR
MarKet fOr DraMa

"I was looking for an elegant, clean, expressive, geometric typeface to give some stability to the playful logo design and typesetting. Futura is clean and perfect yet with lots of character. This suited perfectly to Market for Drama and my design intentions."

Typeface In Use
Futura Book & Bold

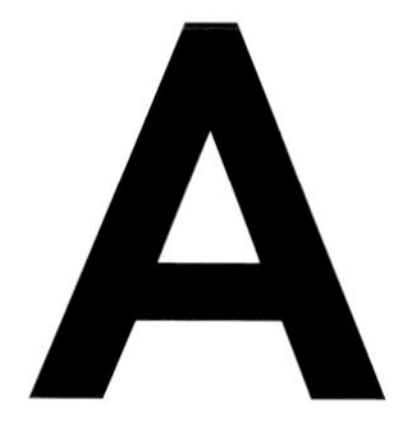

Axel Peemoeller's Favorite Futura Letter Is 'A'.

"Futura Bold A; it is one of the most perfect As."

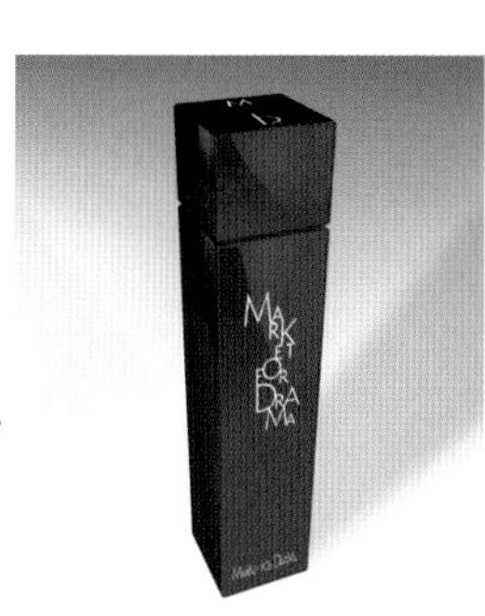

Market for Drama Identity
2009 – Corporate identity, webdesign
Client Market for Drama, NYC
Design Axel Peemoeller

An outstanding, fashionable, euro-style identity with a touch to the cosmetic industry.

Typeface In Use
Avisto (fusion of Futura and Akzidenz Grotesk emerged in the 1930s as Swedish signage)

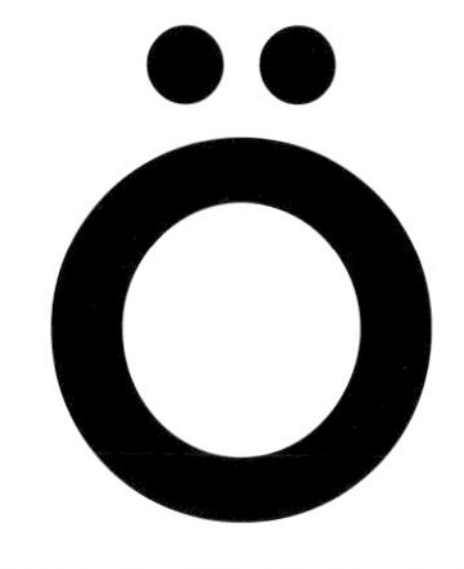

BVD's Favorite Futura Letter Is 'Ö'.

Stories
2007 – Store/Cafe concept, graphic and interior design, naming
Client Turesgruppen
Design BVD (Creative direction - Carin Blidholm Svensson, Design direction - Susanna Nygren Barrett, Graphic design - Johan Andersson, Production - Johanna Haag)

Challenge
To create a strong and totally unique café experience: from concept and name, to graphic profile and packaging. The concept needed to be warm, welcoming, honest and genuine and targeted to young professionals.

Solution
Black, white and stainless steel is blended with warm wood, and the old fashioned café-feeling expressed by things like a board with old, detachable letters and traditional cups and trays. The graphics are clean and simple, but at the same time surprising and playful. The design exudes personality, quality, style and a big city feeling.

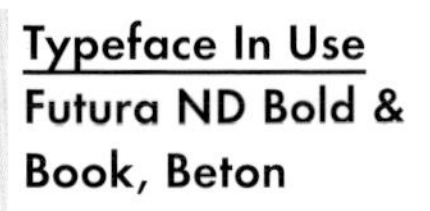

Typeface In Use
Futura ND Bold &
Book, Beton

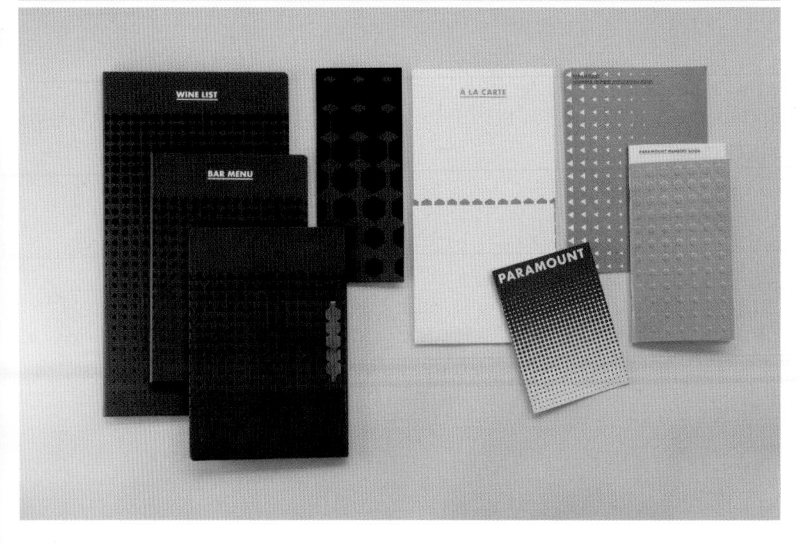

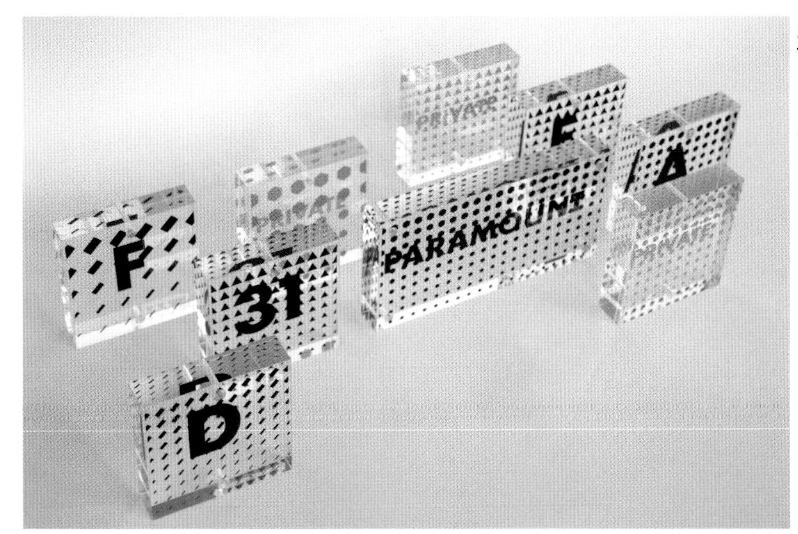

"The architecture of the building relates to the geometric construction of Futura."

Paramount Identity
2009 – Identity, integrated design
Client Paramount
Design Mind Design
Interior design
Tom Dixon, Design Research Studio (www.designresearchstudio.net)

Identity for Paramount, a members' club and event space situated on the top three floors of the 33-story Centre Point building. Centre Point was one of the first skyscrapers in London and has often been described as an example of 1960s Brutalist Architecture. The concept for the identity is simple and based on two main aspects: the architecture of the building and the notion of height. Another strong influence was sixties Op Art, especially the work of Victor Vasarely. The Paramount identity consists of a set of four graduation patterns which express an upwards movement. Each pattern is made from one of four simple shapes (hexagon, triangle, circle and stripe) that can be found in the building or the interior, repeated 33 times to indicate the 33 floors.

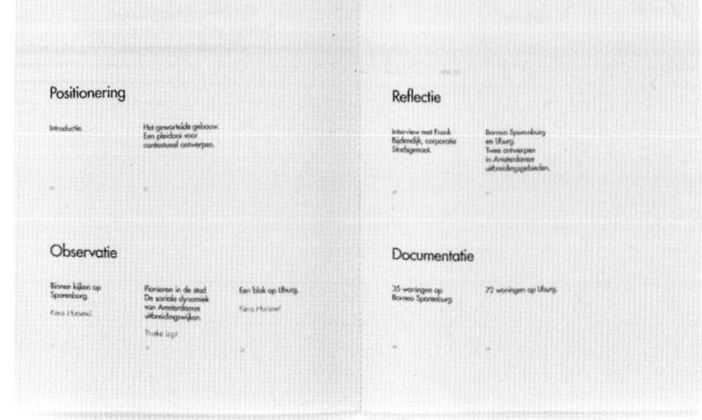

M3H Cahier 01
2009 – Publication
Client M3H Architects, Amsterdam
Design Stout/Kramer

M3H Cahiers **is a series of publications for the Amsterdam based architecture firm M3H. We didn't want to make a "real" book. Like a monography. It would be too much. Instead of one book we came up with the idea of a series of publications. Every issue is about one element of their work.**

Typeface In Use
Futura LT Medium & Light

"Timeless typeface"

Mark Magazine
2006–2008 – Magazine
Client Mark Publishers
Design Lesley Moore

As a basis for the *Mark* typography Lesley Moore selected three typefaces—Futura, Goudy and Gridnik. Based on one of these typefaces, a new typeface was designed for every issue which was used for the headings. By doing this, every issue had its own identity but also clearly belonged to the *Mark* family.

Typeface In Use
Futura Light

"Because of its monumental and pictorial qualities"

BCAD, Benthem Crouwel 1979–2009
2009 – Book
Client Benthem Crouwel Architects, 010 publishers
Design Studio Laucke (Dirk Laucke, Johanna Siebein)

Monograph on the occasion of Benthem Crouwel Architects' 30 years.

Typeface In Use
Futura, AG Buch

"The subtle difference between the solid AG Buch and the 'old-fashioned' Futura, works very well to divide the 'technical part' of the book from the 'poetic part'."

Chronic
2007 – Book
Client Black Cat Publishing
Design Studio Laucke (Dirk Laucke, Johanna Siebein)

Book/Catalog for the exhibition *Chronic* (2007, Chicago).

"This exhibition—the artists' works—discuss the field of tension between colonialism and modernism. The Futura as an icon of western ideas of 'good and beauty' fits very well."

Typeface In Use
Futura Extra Bold

Arctic Paper
2008 – Paper sculpture, photography
Design Shaz Madani

Created as part of a self-initiated proposal for a paper manufacturer. The focus of this campaign was to illustrate the beauty and flexibility of their paper range and showcase how paper can be a great medium for expressing the qualities and the tone of a message as well as bringing images and ideas to life.

Shaz Madani's Favorite Futura Letter Is 'M'.

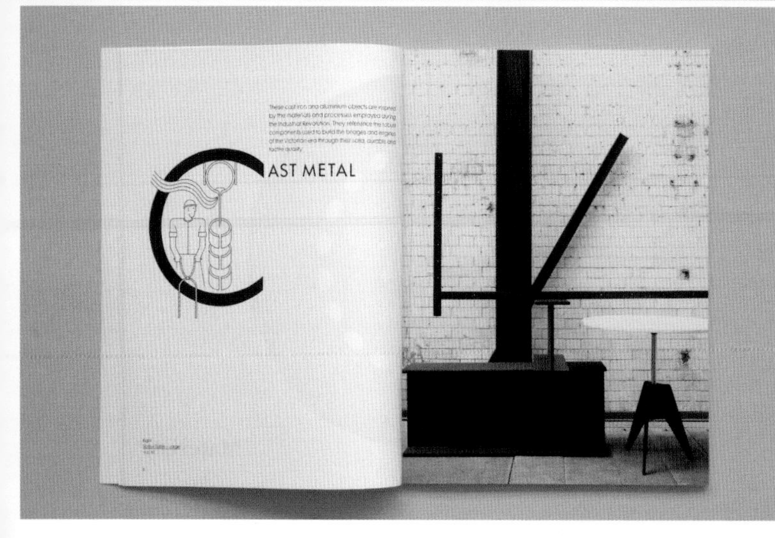

Tom Dixon Catatalogue 2009
2009 – Catalog
Client Tom Dixon
Design Mind Design
Styling Faye Toogood
Illustration Rafael Farias
Photography Henry Bourne

Most furniture designers organize their collection by product groups (chairs, tables, lamps, etc) but this catalog is divided into material groups (steel, copper, brass, etc) as Tom Dixon often produces different items with the same industrial production method. The catalog features large illustrated initial letters showing the various production processes and materials behind the products. The illustrations were inspired by the work of the little known German designer Max Bittrof in the 1920s.

Typeface In Use
Futura Maxi Light,
Hoefler Black

"Futura Maxi Light is one of Tom Dixon's corporate fonts."

Calendar 2009
2009 – Calendar
Design mfsworks

This calendar is a personal whim. Also an attempt to bring and share the passion and love for typography and forms, and to make known its value to those who are not familiar with it. The calendar is designed based on a personal selection of 12 fonts, appearing chronologically according to their year of creation. Some of the fonts chosen have and will have a significant role in the history of this unique technique, others simply are some of my favorites. The shortlist was really complicated, and some were left out... But if anything was clear from the beginning is that Bodoni, Futura and Avant Garde could not be left out.

Typeface In Use
Futura and 11 additional typefaces

"Because it was impossible to design a calendar formed by 12 typefaces and not include these three type-families."

4

Claudio Barandun's Favorite Futura Number Is '4'.

9

Claudio Barandun's Favorite Futura Number Is '9'.

"The geometric shapes of the numbers 4 and 9 fit perfectly well together."

Typeface In Use
Futura Book

49 Meet the Feeling
2008 – Invitation poster
Design Claudio Barandun

This invitation poster was produced in letterpress, which makes the appearance of the letters not only visible, but also haptic.

Typeface In Use
Futura

"For its homogeneous outline, geometric structure and formal neatness. But most of all for its numbers."

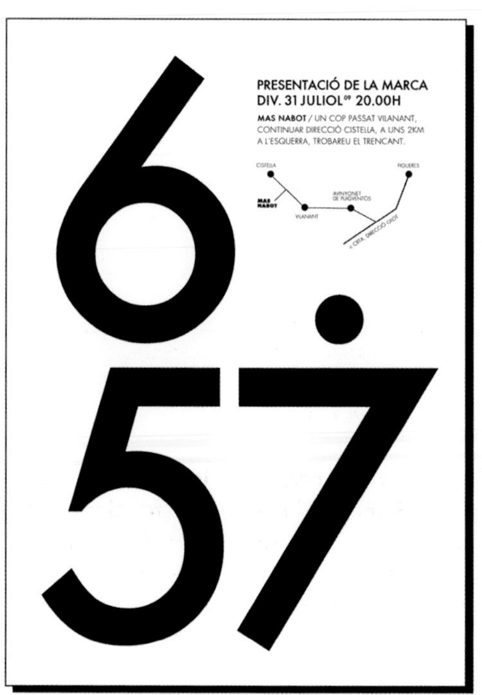

mfsworks' Favorite Futura Number Is '8'.

MIKE
JACKET

MIKE
WAISTCOAT

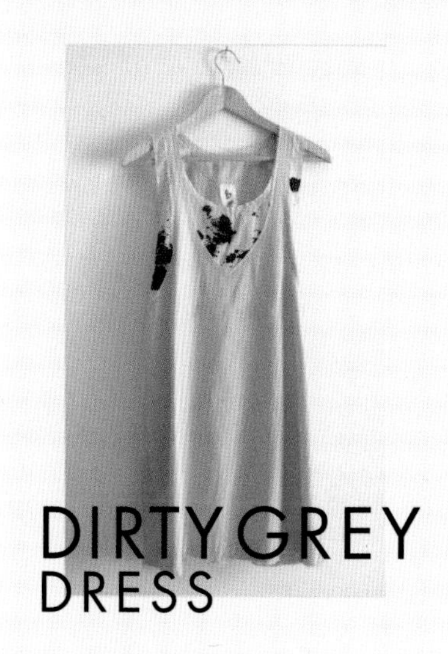

DIRTYGREY
DRESS

DIRTYGREY
SLEEVELESS
T-SHIRT

6.57 Corporate Identity
2009 – Corporate identity, catalog S/S '09
Client 6.57
Design mfsworks

Creation of the corporate identity and design of the catalog of the Spring/Summer '09 collection for clothing brand 6.57. The logo is composed only by numbers and Futura's numbers fitted perfectly to the philosophy and aesthetics of the brand: simple and clean forms, but at the same time combined with a graphic intention, both solid and expressive.

Typeface In Use
Futura Book

"Futura is a modernist typeface which refers to the work of Gerrit Rietveld."

Rietvelds Ranke Ruimtedieren en Andere Creaturen van de Avantgarde (Rietveld's Slender Space Sculptures and Other Creations of the Avantgarde)
2008 – Poster
Client Centraal Museum Utrecht
Design Lesley Moore

The characteristics of the title of the exhibition called for a typographic approach. The poster makes a clear reference to the De Stijl movement without copying it. Rietveld's focus on the spaces "through" and "between" an object is reflected in the emphasis on the "negative" spaces of the letters.

"Futura has in this use a very light attitude, which suited perfectly to the high diving images."

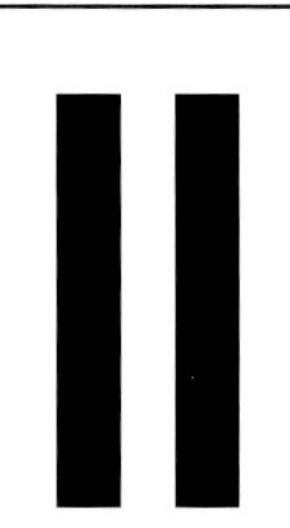

Hi's Favorite Futura Letter Is 'll'.

Monthly Posters for Kulturzentrum Gaswerk, Winterthur
2008 – Poster
Client Kulturzentrum Gaswerk, Winterthur
Design Hi (Megi Zumstein, Claudio Barandun)

While designing this poster, the Olympic Games in Beijing were just on. A good occasion, to put high-divers on the poster of a rock music club.

www.hypetype.co.uk
HYPE TYPE STUDIO
DESIGN + ART DIRECTION

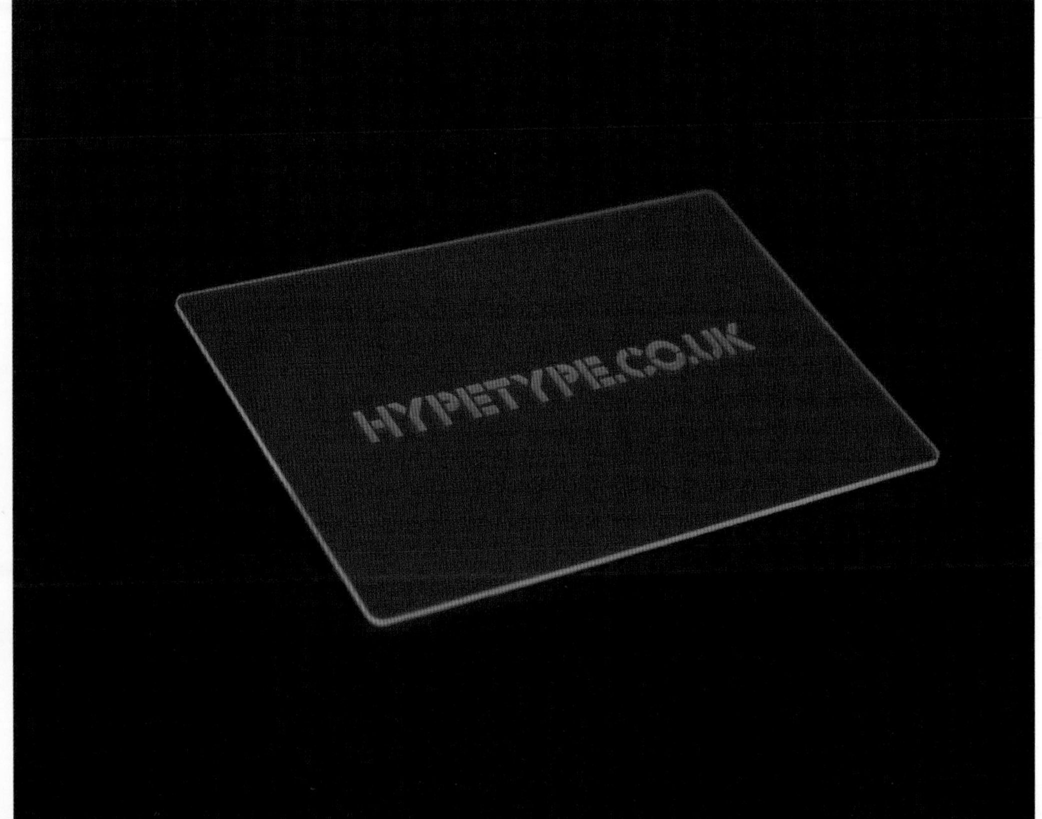
HYPETYPE.CO.UK

Typeface In Use
Futura Stencil

"The geometric shapes, simplicity and clarity of the letters."

Hype Type Studio Self Promotion
2009 – Identity
Design Hype Type Studio (Paul Hutchison)

Like our clients, we have a need for tactile communication which connects. From our stationery to our latest book, materials, printing and application all play an important role in articulating the brand. Careful consideration was given when selecting materials and print techniques, with the aim to promote continuity in a creative way.

Hype Type's Favorite Futura Letter Is 'G'.

"Legibility and a typeface that married well with a serif."

Typeface In Use
Futura Extra Black

SERRAT
2008 – Book
Client Temas de Hoy
Design Studio Astrid Stavro
Photography Mauricio Salinas

This book is an anthology of the work of Spanish folk singer Joan Manuel Serrat. It is a cross between a book of poems and a song book. Chronologically arranged pictures from different moments of Serrat's life serve as chapter dividers. A bold typographic cover in Futura extra black and a series of dust-wrappers made out of giant posters for the deluxe edition help to make the book stand-out and collectable.

Typeface In Use
Futura Book

"This project referred to the 2nd wave of modernism in Los Angeles, Rio de Janeiro, Milano/Torino. Futura was the right typeface to remember to the 1920s, but made also a link to the 1950s design attitudes."

Hi's Favorite Futura Number Is '9'.

Hot Spots 1956–1969, Los Angeles, Rio de Janeiro, Milano/Torino
2009 – Poster design, exhibition walls
Client Kunsthaus Zurich
Design Hi (Megi Zumstein, Claudio Barandun)
Photography Julius Shulman. The Getty Research Institute, J. Paul Getty Trust. Used with permission. Photography Archive, Research Library at the Getty Research Institute.

The 90 degree rotation of the architectural image dissolves the normal perception habit of architectonic spaces, and turns the image into an abstract drawing, which makes it more suitable to represent other works included in the exhibition.

2

Carsten Klein's Favorite Futura Number Is '2'.

Calendar by the Charity
Camden Central Community Umbrella
2004 – A4 fold-out calendar
Client Camden Central Community Umbrella
Design Carsten Klein

Camden Central Community Umbrella is a charitable organization based in Camden Town in London. They wanted to promote themselves and decided to produce a calendar for the year 2004, showing key features of their work.

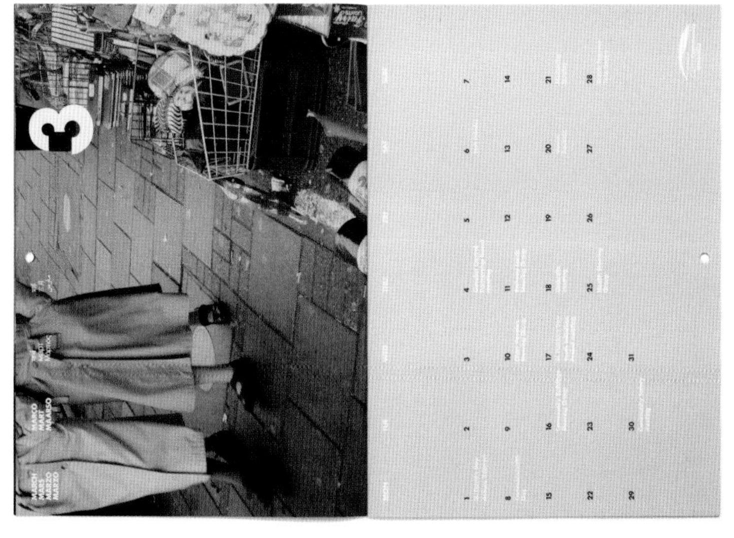

Typeface In Use
Futura Bold

"Black and white photography and a limited budget asked for bold design and simple solutions. We wanted the number of the month to stand out graphically, even at distance. The figures in Futura Bold are both strong and beautiful."

Typeface In Use
Futura Book

Kunst + Vermittlung
2006 – Leporello to introduce the programme of Art Teaching 2006 at Lucerne School of Art and Design
Client Lucerne School of Art and Design
Design Claudio Barandun, Michel Steiner

"There was a bet going on between teachers and us if one would be able to do a nice looking item with this oldschoolish typeface (this was before Futura's renaissance)."

The printing on the blueback poster paper and the special folding technique of this leporello was invented to mix up the backside and the frontside information.

Mišel MATIČEVIĆ

MASQUERADER WITHOUT MASK

26

Neue Mode 8 Magazine
2008 – Editorial design
Client Neue Mode magazine
Design Oliver Daxenbichler

Editorial design for Neue Mode magazine. The magazine's sense is created through the selection of unique images and its distinctive, yet simple layout. The design combines creativity with an uncompromising artistic approach, which aims at post-moderness and straightforwardness.

"The beautiful elegance and the ordinary beauty."

Typeface In Use
Futura LT Extra Bold, Bodoni LT Bold redesigned, ITC Avant Garde Gothic LT Medium

Typeface In Use
Futura

"For its homogeneous outline, geometric structure and formal neatness"

Simbiosi Gift Packaging
2009 – Packaging
Client Simbiosi – Centre de bellesa, benestar i teràpies
Design mfsworks

Redesign of the corporate identity and packaging of the beauty center Simbiosi. Creation of postcards, stationery, and bags for the Christmas campaign of 08/09.

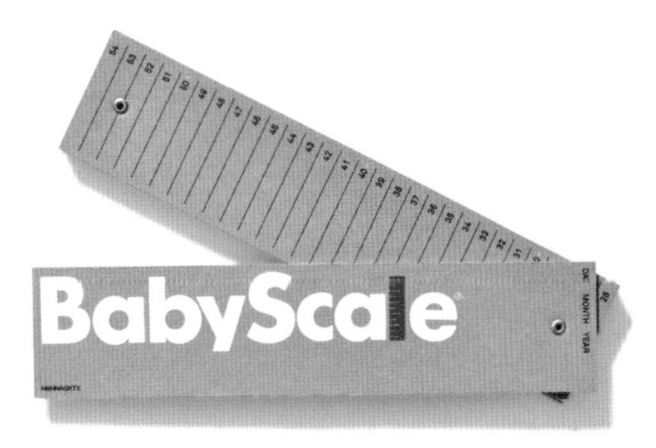

BabyScale
2010 – Packaging, poster, coporate identity, etc.
Client Nonnasixty
Design Studio Astrid Stavro, Grafica
Photography Pablo Martín

A patented portable device for measuring the height of babies and toddlers.

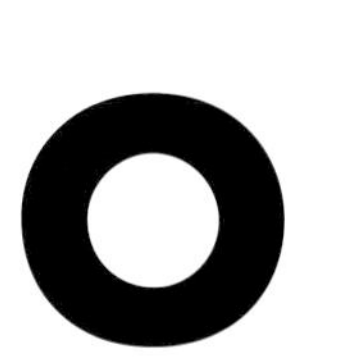

Astrid Stavro & Grafica's Favorite Futura Letter Is 'o'.

"We wanted a very legible and bold typeface but with a warm touch (hence the Babyfutura)."

"We designed a new typeface based on Futura. It is Futura but with slightly rounded edges to make it more baby-like. We called this typeface BabyFutura. The typeface was designed by Oscar Germade."

Typeface In Use
BabyFutura (customised Futura)

Wedding Invitation
2007 – Invitation
Client Mrs. Catriona Pollock, Mr. Stephen Wood
Design Carsten Klein

This wedding invitation makes use of a very traditional invitation in which the father of the bride announces the wedding of his daughter. The arrangement of type and the font itself resemble a book cover. Type was screen-printed onto an A5-sized piece of ply-wood, the shape and feel of which enhances the overall feel of a book.

a

Carsten Klein's Favorite Futura Letter Is 'a'.

"The overall feel of the invite is meant to resemble a book cover, which then needed a no-fuss, bold typeface. It was also essential to steer away from the ornamental standards of typical wedding invitations. The bold and geometric nature Futura met this criteria perfectly."

marie —————————— laure hoedemakers

Marie–Laure Hoedemakers
Landschapsarchitect

J.F. Berghoefplantsoen 15 —— 1064 DE Amsterdam —— Telefoon +31 (0)6 2473 6184
mail@m–lh.com —— www.m–lh.com

marie —————————— laure hoedemakers

KvK: 34255426 —— BTW: NL 1565.81.760.B01
ABN Amro Rekening: 49.29.79.510

Marie-Laure Hoedemakers
Landscape Architect
2008 – Corporate identity, stationery
Client Marie-Laure Hoedemakers
Design Carsten Klein

The rather lengthy name *Marie-Laure Hoedemakers* and especially the hyphen in the first name was originally considered a problem. Until we took that hyphen, stretched it and made that the main feature of Marie-Laure's identity. So far that the hyphen becomes the dominant feature on matters such as postcards, and even the website address www.m-lh.com. This plain and simple solution doesn't even need support by, for example, use of color and instead works best as black and white, type-only.

Typeface In Use
Futura Bold,
ITC Franklin Gothic Book

"The exaggeration of the hyphen in 'Marie-Laure' had to be held together by a strong and bold typeface, which Futura Bold seemed to fit this bill. It continues the graphic nature of the long 'landscape hyphen'."

"From Manifiesto Futura, Social Rocker Club was born. Created to search for talents and collaborations. We wanted both brands to bond."

Typeface In Use
Futura Bold

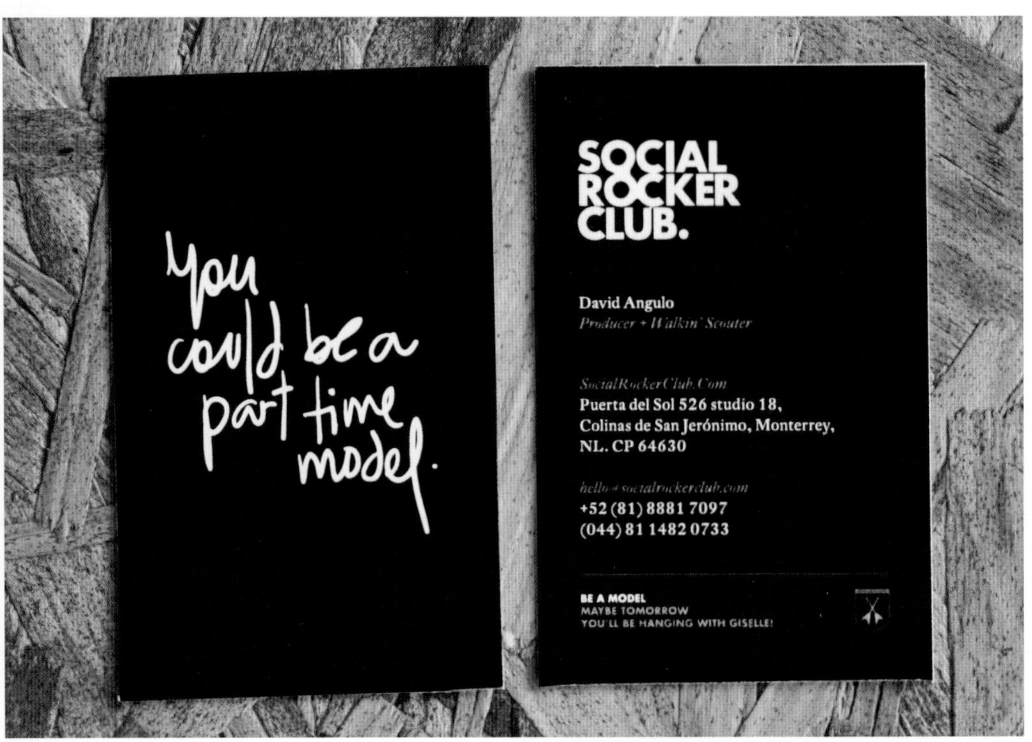

Social Rocker Club
2008 – Logo, corporate identity
Design Manifiesto Futura

Social Rocker Club was created as a brand that would help us find hidden talents for photo shoots. We needed something that could work as a business card/flyer and invitation; that's why our result doesn't involve a special or expensive printer solution. Final size 5x9 cm, one ink (black) each side.

K

Manifiesto Futura's Favorite Futura Letter Is 'K'.

Manifiesto Futura Identity
2008 – Corporate identity
Design Manifiesto Futura

Representing the future in past times, something without an ending cycle.

Typeface In Use
Futura Bold

"At first we only wanted to be called Futura, so the typeface was a must. But who are we kidding? We love Futura."

T

Manifiesto Futura's Favorite Futura Letter Is 'T'.

CINEMA EXP
RESSIONNISTE
ALLEMAND
AU KINO DU
4 AU 10 AVRIL
19H 21H
LE CABINET
DU DOCTEUR
CALIGARI RO
BERT WIENE
1919

CINEMA EXP
RESSIONNISTE
ALLEMAND
AU KINO DU
4 AU 10 AVRIL
19H 21H
LE CABINET
DU DOCTEUR
CALIGARI RO
BERT WIENE
1919

CINEMA EXP
RESSIONNISTE
ALLEMAND
AU KINO DU
4 AU 10 AVRIL
19H 21H
LE CABINET
DU DOCTEUR
CALIGARI RO
BERT WIENE
1919

German Expressionism
Rétrospective
2008 – Corporate
design
Design Xavier Barrade

Typeface In Use
Futura, Aardcover

Visual identity for the theater *Kino*, for a retrospective on German expressionism movies. Two typefaces, a Futura (modern) and an Aardcover (standing for the spirit of German expressionism) meet, face, and stand with each other on the different media to speak about the retrospective, and the theme of schizophrenia— omnipresent in *Le Cabinet du Docteur Caligari*, first movie to be screened.

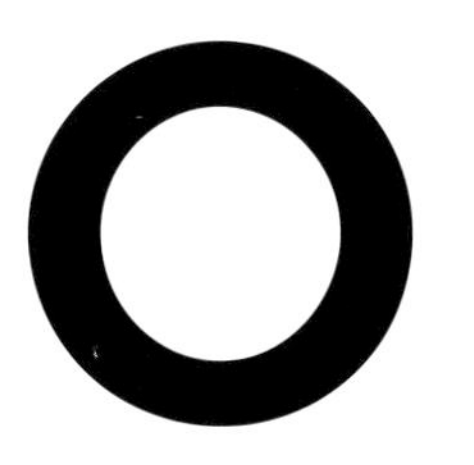

Xavier Barrade's
Favorite Futura Letter
Is 'O'.

a

Mind Design's Favorite
Futura Letter Is 'a'.

Typeface In Use
Futura Bold & Light

"Futura is the Artek corporate font used on all their communication."

pølse stol/ sausage chair/

artek

Artek oy ab
Lemuntie 3 - 5 B
FI -00510 Helsinki
Finland

info@artek.fi
www.artek.fi

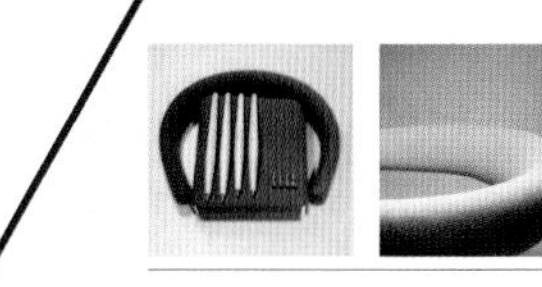

Nanna Ditzel (1923 - 2005)

Four high quality turned oak legs, a back and a seat. The sausage chair is so clever and simple in construction that it is a wonder that no one else had thought of it before...

Easy to ship, to construct and to store, Nanna Ditzel's triumph is an extremely comfortable easy chair that sits happily in hotel lobbies, restaurants and bars, or will perform just as well in a domestic interior.

Nanna Ditzel
Born in Copenhagen, Denmark in 1923. Nanna trained as a cabinetmaker before studying at the School of Arts and Crafts and the Royal Academy of Fine Arts in Copenhagen. She graduated in furniture design in 1946 and established her own design studio together with Jørgen Ditzel the same year and continued to work in the design sector until shortly before her death in Copenhagen in June 2005.

From the start of her career in the post war years, she was always challenged by new materials and new techniques. Nanna worked in various materials such as fibre glass, wickerwork and foam rubber and in various disciplines such as cabinetmaking, jewellery, tableware, applied art and textiles.

In the 1950s she experimented with split level floor seating. From 1968 to 1986 she lived in London, establishing the international furniture house Interspace in Hampstead with Kurt Heide.

Among her designs in continuous production are jewellery for Georg Jensen, textiles for Kvadrat and furniture for Fredericia, Kvist, Getama amongst others.

Nanna Ditzel has exhibited internationally at One Woman exhibitions in Amsterdam, Berlin, New York, Vienna, London, Stockholm, Milan, Glasgow, Manchester, Reykjavik, Paris and Denmark.

Awarded numerous international prizes, including, in 1990, the Gold Medal in the International Furniture Design Competition, Japan, for her Bench for Two (Fredericia). Elected Honourable Royal Designer in London in 1996 and awarded the Lifelong Artists' Grant by the Danish Ministry of Culture in 1998.

<u>Artek – Sausage Chair Poster</u>
2006 – Poster
<u>Client</u> Artek
<u>Design</u> Mind Design (Creative direction - Holger Jacobs)
<u>Photography</u> Metz+Racine

Poster to advertise the re-launch of Nanna Ditzel's *Sausage Chair* at the furniture fair in Milan. The shape of the *Sausage Chair*'s back-rest inspired the idea of using balloons as a simple but effective props in the photoshoot for the poster. The back of the poster repeats an angled bar in the Danish lettering as typographic element.

BLAST OF SILENCE

AUGUST

Die neue Hamburger Schule war um dramatische Spannungsbögen und groß angelegte Epikkonzepte ja nie wirklich verlegen. „House is a feeling", heißt es da dann gerne. Ein Glück, dass man bei SOLOMUN und STIMMING nie in der Cheesyness-Falle landet und dass obwohl hier Emotionalität doch großgeschrieben wird und man sich geflissentlich einem gewissen Raver-Pathos zu versagen weigert. Man geht schließlich immer noch aus, um sich bewegen zu lassen, wa? Bewegung auf hohem Niveau, genau. DIYNAMIC, das Label von SOLOMUN, hat sich in den letzten Jahren aber auch zur stilbildenden Referenzgröße in Sachen Breitwandhouse gemausert: Ravig an der Oberfläche prickelnd, fahren hier Stringwellen noch ungebremst durch die Endorphinzentrale und sorgen dafür, dass trotz allem Willen zur Abfahrt profunde Musikalität nicht auf der Strecke bleibt. Das 2009 veröffentlichte Debüt-Album "Reflections" von STIMMING rührte entsprechend nicht nur die Gemüter des gemeinen Ravers, sondern auch die kalten Herzen des analytisch geschulten Musikjournalisten, der Hand in Hand mit ersterem, tränenbenetzten Auges und in verschwitzter Montur den 25jährigen Hamburger vom Dancefloor aus bejubelte. DE:BUG, GROOVE – alle lieben STIMMING ob seiner Dramaturgie, seiner perfekten Produktion und natürlich seinem treffsicheren Händchen für's große Gefühl. SOLOMUN, der sich auf diesem Gebiet besonders auskennt, hat sich ja mittlerweile auch durch Releases auf 4:TWENTY, COMPOST und SONAR KOLLEKTIV, sowie den legendären Nummern auf LIEBE*DETAIL zu einem der wichtigsten Figuren jener klassisch geschulten Housefraktion entwickelt, für die Deepness immer schon vor ästhetischer Reduktion stand. Die neue Hamburger Schule. Besser als jede andere...

BLAST OF SILENCE
ROLAND APPEL

SOLOMUN STIMMING *live*

{ DIYNAMIC / HAMBURG }
DER BRANE

1 YEAR

8 AUG DIE REGISTRATUR

2008 2009

BLAST OF SILENCE

BLAST OF SILENCE
ROLAND APPEL

RADIO SLAVE

{ REKIDS / BERLIN }
DER BRANE

18 MÄRZ

DIE REGISTRATUR

und wenn Berlin nicht untergeht, wird auch PHONIQUE weiter scheinen.

JUNI

ÂME, das sind die Guten. Nicht umsonst heißen die ‚Seele'. Diese ist nämlich gar nicht so einfach zu bewahren in diesem Geschäft der Nacht, wo jeder darauf aus ist, sie einem auszusaugen. Seele ist es jedoch, die Kristian und Frank ihrer Konkurrenz voraushaben, das, weswegen ihr Wiedererkennungswert trotz unterschiedlichster Ansätze ungemein hoch bleibt. Das hört man in ihren Sets, wie dem sagenhaften „Coast 2 Coast"-Mix, vor allem aber in den eigenen Produktionen der Karlsruher. Deshalb fällt es NachÂMErn (hihi) auch so unglaublich schwer, den Sound der Beiden zu kopieren. Man denke nur an die tausend gescheiterten Versuche, ein zweites „Rej" zu erzeugen. Immer einen Schritt voraus, haben ÂME 2009, nachdem man House wieder salonfähig gebügelt hatte, schließlich eine erneute öffentliche Reflexion des Minimaldiskurses vom Zaun gebrochen. Nene, nicht Minimal wie die schmatzenden Halblinge da draußen es kennen, Minimal, wie es die Opas gehört haben. Deshalb nennt sich die Kompilation, die in Zusammenarbeit mit Henrik Schwarz und Dixon entstand, auch „The Grandfather Paradox", ein Rückgriff auf die notwendigen Schwierigkeiten, denen man begegnen würde, könnte man in der Zeit zurückreisen und seinen Großvater töten bevor dieser mit Oma anzubandeln in der Lage war (womit die eigentlich Existenz ja ad absurdum geführt wäre). Das auf Minimal-Musik übertragen muss ja nicht heißen, die Gründerväter zu exekutieren, kann aber im Idealfall das Bewusstsein dafür schärfen, wie unser als gegeben hingenommener Status Quo im Kontext von Jungs, wie Steve Reich, Conrad Schnitzler oder Moondog erscheint. Das Ergebnis ist so unterhaltsam und frisch, wie didaktisch wertvoll. Umso großartiger, dass die modernsten Überlegungen zur Seele kontemporärer Clubklänge weder aus Berlin, noch aus Detroit zu kommen scheinen. Karlsruhe ru-

BLAST OF SILENCE
ROLAND APPEL

PHO NIQUE

{ POKERFLAT/ BERLIN }
DER BRANE

9 MAI

DIE REGISTRATUR

1

2

4

3

5

8

Levi's® 501® worn by
[1] Roland Appel [2] Radioslave [3] Solomon [4] Stimming [5] Der Brane [6] Phonique [7] Ame [8] Mirko Borsche

6

7

Typeface In Use
Futura Medium

BLAST OF SILENCE THE MAG
2009 – Editorial
Client Die Registratur
Design Bureau Mirko Borsche

Roland Appel was the initiator of the legendary partyseries ***BLAST OF SILENCE***, a housemusic event with various wellknown DJs. Bureau Mirko Borsche was commissioned to design a magazine, where the DJs were presented.

"It's simple and effective."

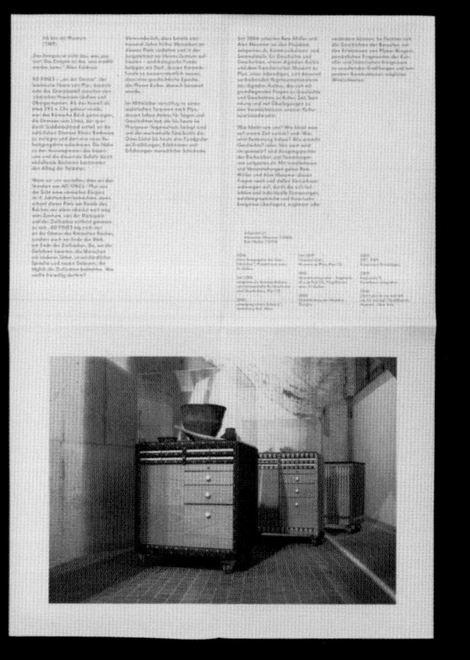

"The strict arrangement of the exhibition display-cases inspired to use a sharp-edged and geometric typeface like Futura."

Poster TMP
2010 – Poster
Client Kunstraum Winterthur, Winterthur, CH
Design Gloor & Jandl

This poster is part of a whole variety of printed matter for an offspace art gallery near Zurich. The printed exposure of featuring artists at the moment appears as an all-purpose poster. This strict and multifunctional adaption arises from the low budget and allows to operate within short-term commissions.

Typeface In Use
Futura Book

SCHMUCK
UND OBJEKTE DER
ALLTAGSKULTUR

(SCHMUCK (ER-)FINDEN)

BEWIRB DICH

HOCHSCHULE PFORZHEIM
FAKULTÄT FÜR GESTALTUNG
HOLZGARTENSTRASSE 36
D-75175 PFORZHEIM
TEL. 07231/286727
HTTP://WWW.GESTALTUNG.
HS-PFORZHEIM.DE

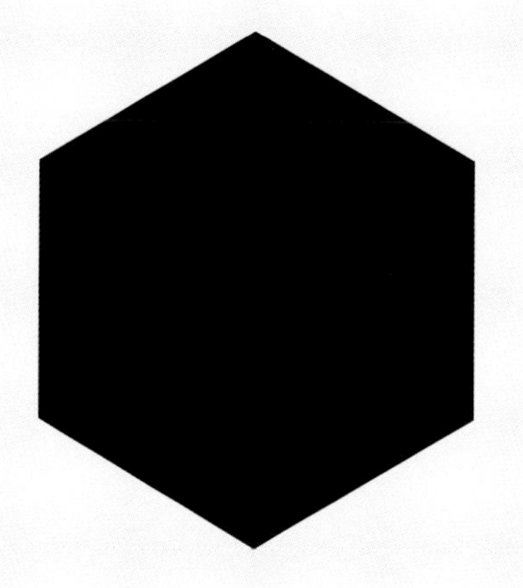

Schmuck
2008 – Poster set
Client Jewelry Studies at Pforzheim University, Faculty of Design
Design Felix Müthe

Image campaign for Jewelry Studies at Pforzheim University. A set of two posters—one contains text, the other is a stencil form that frames the background where the posters are put on. The message is that everything could be jewelry or everyday objects, you just have to sharpen your eyesight—Schmuck (er-)finden!

Typeface In Use
Futura Book

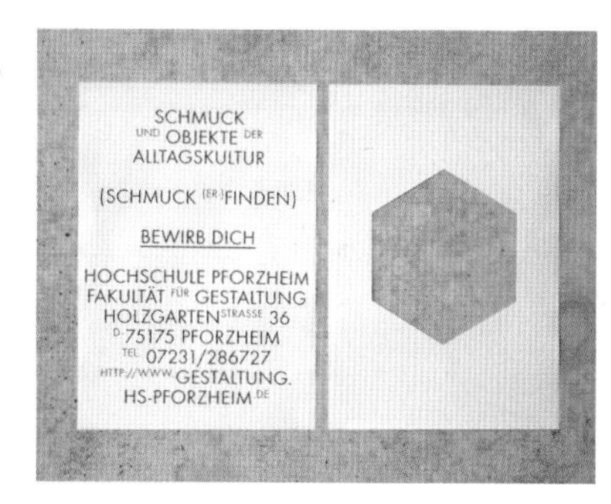

9

Felix Müthe's Favorite Futura Number Is '9'.

I WANT TO
LAUGH,
I WANT TO
CRY.

LAUGH/CRY
2008
Design Oliver Daxenbichler

Expressional T-shirt design incorporating the diversity of broken hearts. Designed to get over a broken heart fast.

Typeface In Use
Customized Futura LT Extra Bold

O

Oliver Daxenbichler's Favorite Futura Letter Is 'O'.

Typeface In Use
Futura LT Extra Bold

ENFIN.
2009 – Exhibition identity and branding
Client Neue Mode galleries
Design Oliver Daxenbichler

Identity and exhibition design for the *Neue Mode* galleries opening. Collateral includes flyers, press and signage.

"The typeface expresses the modern eliminating non-essential elements."

THE
HUMAN
LEAGUE

REPRODUCTION/1979
TRAVELOGUE/1980
DARE/1981
LOVE&DANCING/1982
FASCINATION/1983
HYSTERIA/1984
CRASH/1986
ROMANTIC/1990
OCTOPUS/1995
SECRETS/2001

Typeface In Use
Cutomized Futura LT
Extra Bold

The Human League Tribute Poster
2007 – Poster
Design Oliver Daxenbichler

A1 screen-printed poster for the ever popular British synthpop band The Human League. I chose to enter into the spirit of their first #1 UK album *Dare* and designed the poster as a bold simple two-color design in tribute to the album artwork.

"Futura has an appearance of efficiency and forwardness."

LOOSE
BUILD
SHIPS.

LOOSE LIPS BUILD SHIPS, PLANES, BRIDGES,
HOUSES, CITIES, COUNTRIES, STORIES, IDEAS.

FREEDOM OF SPEECH. THE FIRST FREEDOM.

Experimental Jetset 0/20

Loose Lips Build Ships
Thoughts on Democracy
2008 – Poster series
Design Experimental Jetset

Not being big fans of Norman Rockwell, we were a bit hesitant when The Wolfsonian, a museum based in Miami, approached us to participate in "Thoughts on Democracy", a poster exhibition revolving around a series of paintings that Rockwell created in 1943, based on Roosevelt's "Four Freedoms" speech from 1941. (The freedoms addressed in that speech were "freedom of speech", "freedom of religion", "freedom from want", and "freedom from fear"). In short, The Wolfsonian asked a group of artists (including us) to design a poster referring to the theme of "Thoughts on Democracy". (In the exact words of the museum, "the exhibition will comprise of posters created by sixty leading contemporary artists and designers, invited by The Wolfsonian to create a new graphic design inspired by American illustrator Norman Rockwell's 'Four Freedoms', which were recently gifted to the museum by Leonard A. Lauder").

Typeface In Use
Futura

The reason we eventually decided to join the exhibition had a lot to do with the fact that it was Wim Crouwel who invited us to participate, which made it hard to refuse. Also, the crew at The Wolfsonian sounded really enthusiastic, so we decided to give it a try. As we already confessed, we didn't really like Rockwell's original posters, and we were initially thinking about creating a poster that would question this whole American notion of freedom, for example by referring to Noam Chomsky's "Fifth Freedom". That was our first impulse. But at the same time, we didn't want to come across as being cynical about freedom. We felt we had to take into consideration people like Wim Crouwel, the generation that lived through the

Second World War, people for who this whole American notion of freedom really meant something. More importantly, we realized that what made us wary of Rockwell's posters was not so much the notion of freedom, but more the notion of propaganda. So we decided to make a poster about propaganda instead. The slogan "Loose Lips Build Ships" is a collision of two iconic WWII posters: the "Freedom of Speech" poster as painted by Rockwell, and the "Loose Lips May Sink Ships" poster, which was the US Office of War Information's attempt to limit the possibility of people inadvertently giving useful information to enemy spies.

"Loose Lips Build Ships" is a contradiction of "Loose Lips Sink Ships", but at the same time an affirmation of "Freedom of Speech". By creating a slight friction between these two iconic slogans, we wanted to show our uneasiness with the whole concept of propaganda. We originally designed a completely typographic poster, just bearing the slogan "Loose Lips Build Ships". At the last moment, we decided to replace the word "Lips" with an actual image of lips. We thought the image of the lips fitted quite well with the idea of speaking, with the theme of freedom of speech. But we still aren't exactly sure if we made the right decision here. Maybe the concept, of two clashing slogans, would have been clearer if executed purely typographical. Anyway. It's too late now. The poster, 16x20 inch, was exhibited at The Wolfsonian between July 5 and December 7, 2008. Thanks to Cathy Leff, Donna Carter and Tim Hossler of The Wolfsonian.

JEROME SAINT-LOUBERT BIE
EXPOSE 13 AFFICHES DE

FRANCIS BAUDEVIN
DOCUMENTATION CELINE DUVAL
DANIEL EATOCK
EXPERIMENTAL JETSET
CHRISTOPH KELLER
MEVIS & VAN DEURSEN
JONATHAN MONK
DAVE MULLER
REGULAR
YANN SERANDOUR
STRIPE / JON SUEDA & GAIL SWANLUND
JIAN-XING TOO
VIER5

DU 15 SEPTEMBRE AU 31 OCTOBRE 2007
A L'ATELIER CARDENAS BELLANGER
43 RUE QUINCAMPOIX, 75004 PARIS

DU MARDI AU SAMEDI
DE 11 HEURES A 19 HEURES

VERNISSAGE LE SAMEDI 15 SEPTEMBRE
A PARTIR DE 18 HEURES

AFFICHE EXPERIMENTAL JETSET 2007

JET
SET
AIR
BOMB
EURO
LINE

Typeface In Use
Futura Condensed
Bold

Check One Two
2009 – Flyer, poster design
Client Check One Two
Design Robi Jõeleht

"I love the look of Futura."

Robi Jõeleht's Favorite Futura Letter Is 'R'.

Clashment
2008 – Flyer, poster design
Client Clashment
Design Robi Jõeleht

Typeface In Use
Futura Medium & Bold

c

Everything Design's Favorite Futura Letter Is 'c'.

Breast Cancer Foundation Street Appeal
2009 – Campaign, poster design
Client New Zealand Breast Cancer Foundation
Design Everything Design (Jason Saunders, Gareth Ormerod)

As part of the work we did to promote Breast Cancer Action month in October we designed these fluorescent posters to advertise The New Zealand Breast Cancer Foundation's Street Appeal. Media owners Adshel were so impressed with them that they contacted the Foundation to say they were a perfect demonstration of what their channel can deliver in terms of cut through, high visibility and effective communication of key messages. In fact they were so impressed that they offered to come on board as a Foundation sponsor and provide the Breast Cancer Foundation with free Adshel placements in the future.

Typeface In Use
Futura Bold

"We made Futura the primary corporate font for the Foundation in brand guidelines that we developed earlier in 2009."

THE FUTUREHEADS
2004 – Record packaging, campaign
Client 679 Recordings
Design Big Active

Big Active were commissioned to create a strong defining image and distinctive visual identity for the Futureheads' debut album package and integrated promotional campaign.

"We used this typeface throughout because it was distinctive and appropriate to the project"

Typeface In Use
Futura-heads (Based upon customized Futura redrawn and remixed by Big Active)

MINGLE
WITH
STRANGERS.
GIVE AND TAKE.
START
SOMETHING
NEW.
ACCESS TO
THE CITY.

OPEN CITY.

PARTICIPATE.
CONTRIBUTE.
URBAN
CHALLENGES.
MAKE
YOUR CITY.

OPEN CITY.

SAFE AND
DIVERSE.
EXPRESSING
IDENTITY.
COMMUNITY.
THE CITY
IS YOURS.

OPEN CITY.

ACTIVE
CITIZENS.
SENSE OF
BELONGING.
COLLECTIVE.
MAKE THE CITY
WORK.

OPEN CITY.

SAFE HAVEN.
EMPOWERING
MIGRANTS.
REFUGE.
MAKING
PLANS FOR
A BETTER
TOMORROW.

OPEN CITY.

M

Stout/Kramer's Favorite Futura Letter Is 'M'.

International Architecture Biennale Rotterdam, Open City Campaign
2009 – Campaign
Client International Architecture Biennale Rotterdam
Design Stout/Kramer

The campaign for the International Architecture Biennale Rotterdam contains seven text posters plus one announcement poster. The text fragments are collected from different resources. Each poster is referring to a different theme of the Biennale.

4th International Architecture Biennale Rotterdam
Open City: Designing Coexistence
25 Sep 2009 - 10 Jan 2010 Rotterdam-Amsterdam
www.iabr.nl

THE CITY
IS A STAGE.
COMMON
ACTION.
CONNECTING
ALL THE
NETWORKS.

OPEN CITY.

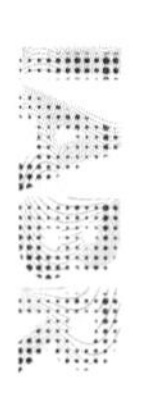

Typeface In Use
Futura Medium

"Strong in simplicity yet stylish."

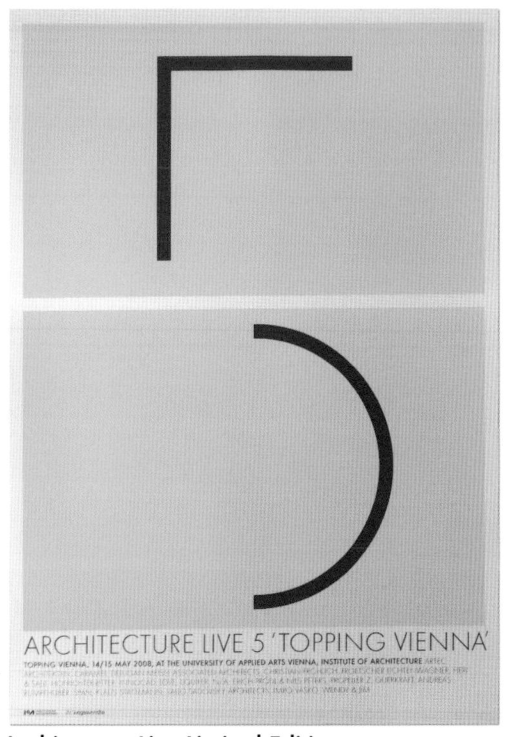

"The simplicity and strength of the letter shapes of Futura lent them to be applied to this design."

Architecture Live Limited Edition
Screen-printed Posters
2007–2009 – A1 poster series
Client Institute of Architecture,
University of Applied Arts Vienna
Design Paulus M. Dreibholz
Printing Master-printer Olivia Sautreuil

Architecture Live is an event where established and up-and-coming architects are invited to conduct workshops with the students of the University of Applied Arts Vienna. The results of these workshops are then exhibited and published in a magazine. *The Architecture Live* limited edition posters were designed to be handed out to the people running the workshops as a thank you and memory. The Institute of Architecture provides an experimental education and has a strong appreciation for the Constructivists and Futurists. The basic layout establishes the posters as a series, with the deconstructed numerals giving the posters their individual signature.

SpringerWienNewYork edition:'angewandte

99+ IOA STUDIOS
HADID LYNN
PRIX SELECTED
STUDENT WORKS
2004–8 Design =
Thinking

"UNIVERSITIES SHOULD NOT BEAR THE TRAIN OF EXISTING POWERS, BUT CARRY THE TORCH IN FRONT OF THOSE POWERS"

Typeface In Use
Futura URW

Paulus M. Dreibholz's Favorite Futura Number Is '6'.

Institute of Architecture (IoA)
2009 – Yearbook
Client Institute of Architecture, University of Applied Arts Vienna
Design Paulus M. Dreibholz

The yearbook is an annual publication published by the Institute of Architecture at the University of Applied Arts Vienna. It showcases the projects undertaken and accomplished by the students of the three design studios run by Zaha Hadid, Greg Lynn and Wolf D. Prix. The work is of a highly experimental nature pushing boundaries of the field. The object itself, with its open binding, black on black foiling and black thread becomes an austere sculpture contrasting the highly glossy dust jacket that's wrapped around it.

"Futura offers a range of weights and good contrast and in this project everything was about contrast. Strong colors on the dust jacket, black only inside. Glossy-coated outside, uncoated inside. Thick endpapers, thin stock for the interior. Bold future for headlines, thin cuts for the remaining text, etc."

EFEMÉRIDE

2009–2010 – Cultural Newspaper
Client Travessa da Ermida
Design -nada-

Travessa da Ermida is a project that includes a small gallery housed in an old chapel, a jewelry workshop and a wine bar, all in a small alley in Belém, Lisbon. This project aims to bring all these disciplines closer to the general public through a free publication. ***EFEMÉRIDE*** is a free quarterly cultural newsletter/newspaper that features small articles about art, design, jewelry, wines and a poster of an invited artist. A1 sheet folded into A3 with a print run of 12,500 and distributed around the country in select places like museums and galleries, bars, schools, restaurants, etc...

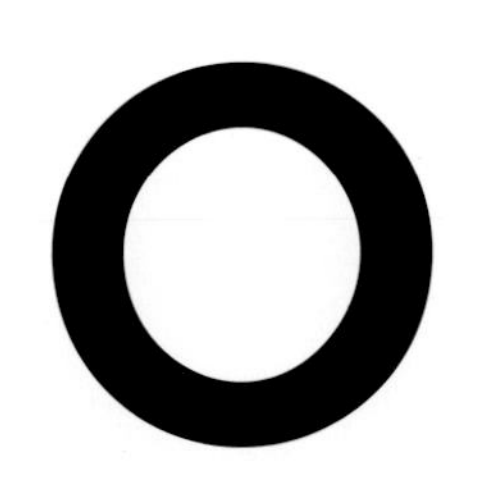

Typeface In Use
Futura Black, Melior & custom typeface

"Clean and bold as we wanted."

-nada-'s Favorite Futura Letter Is 'O'.

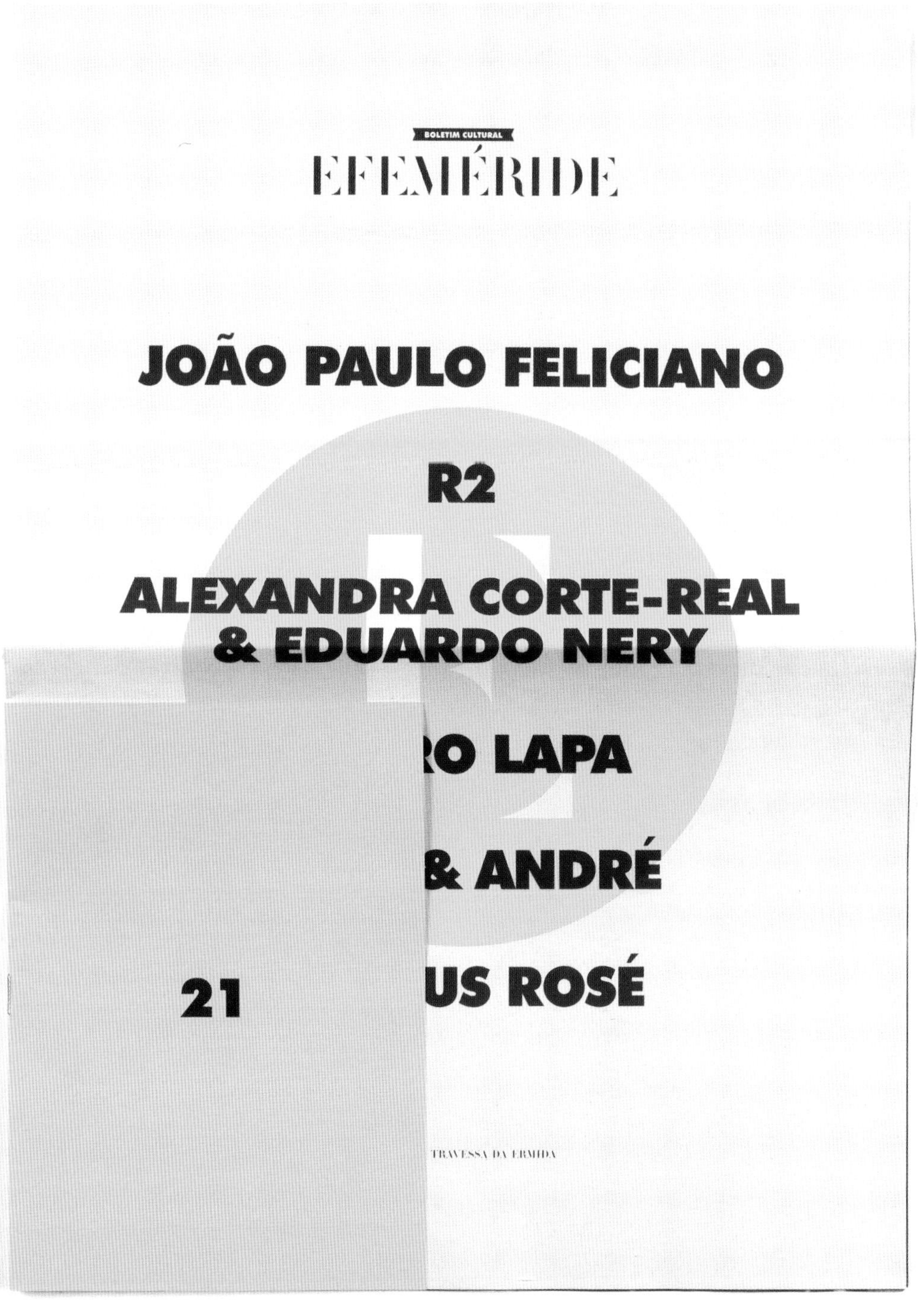

BOLETIM CULTURAL

EFEMÉRIDE

JOÃO PAULO FELICIANO

R2

ALEXANDRA CORTE-REAL
& EDUARDO NERY

RO LAPA

& ANDRÉ

21

US ROSÉ

TRAVESSA DA ERMIDA

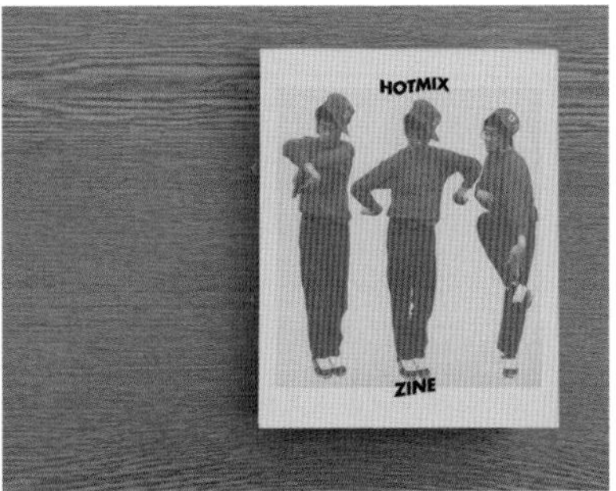

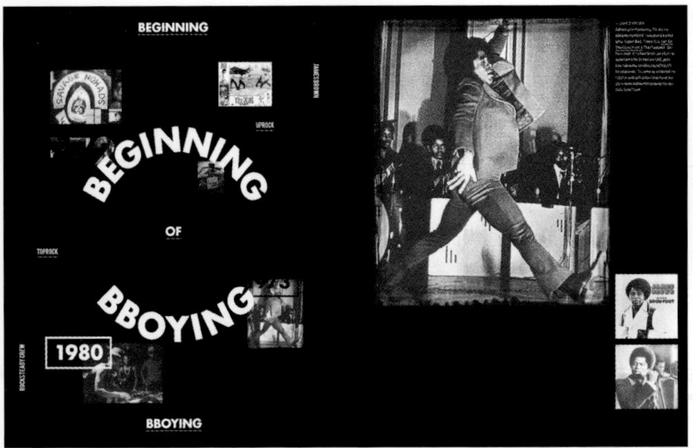

Hotmix Zine
2010 – Corporate identity
Design Filip Matejícek

Hotmix is a magazine about breakdance and streetdance. It's published in Prague to support the Czech dance scene.

N

Filip Matejicek's Favorite Futura Letter Is 'N'.

"Due to its massive ductus in a bold, which has the ability to hold shape in the twisted form."

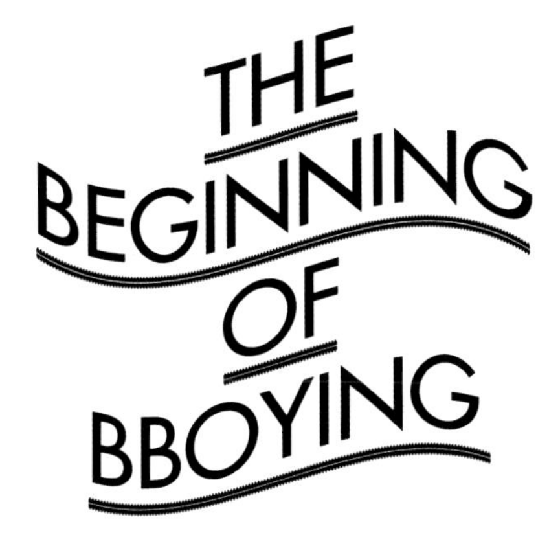

Typeface In Use
Futura CE Bold

"Elegant and luxurious"

Make_Studio's
Favorite Futura Letter
Is 'N'.

3D Type
2010
Design Make_Studio

Building on 3D type for our portfolio, we have taken a few logos that we produced as well as the original Avant Garde magazine logo in order to show our clients a different dimension to type.

Maria Luisa Fall/Winter 2010-2011
Lookbook
2010 – Illustration
Client Maria Luisa, Paris
Design Ahonen & Lamberg

Abstract and surreal but chic and glamorous landscape.

"Futura's beautiful extra bold-cut with good readability is a great base for this kind of illustrative typography."

DasArts Meets De Bank
2007 – Poster
Client DasArts Foundation, Amsterdam
Design Niels Schrader, Eike Dingler

Typeface In Use
Futura BQ, Baskerville Book BQ

"The Futura typeface was part of the client's corporate design."

"As the invitation was made from metal it needed a strong legible typeface, a bit machine-like, though still with elegance and softness to it from keeping the invitation away for becoming too industrial—hence the choice of the elegant and slick Futura."

Man VS Machine
2009 – Invitation
Client BLAAK
Design Thorbjørn Ankerstjerne

Typeface In Use
Futura STD Bold, Heavy & Medium

The invitation measures 9x16 cm and is made from 1mm steel mesh. The text is printed onto transparent film which then has been coated with a layer of varnish on both sides. This rather masculine and "hands-on" invitation was produced by hand in 500 editions and was made for the London based fashion label BLAAK's Autumn/Winter 2009–2010 collection.

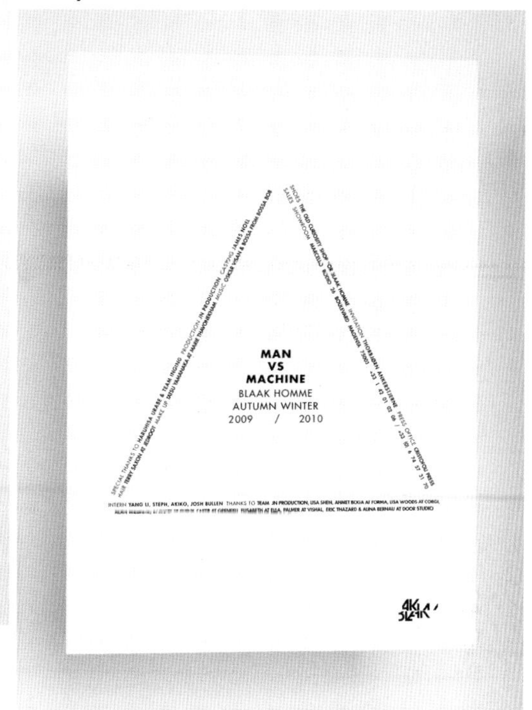

"I wanted the credit list to have the same look and feel as the invitation."

Credit List

As mentioned, I wanted the credit list to reflect the bold and direct style of the invitation. The triangular layout was inspired by one of BLAAK's printed garments.

RUN
DEM
CREW

BEN
DRURY
&
DIZZEE
RASCAL

KEEP ON
RUNNING

MARK BAJADE, age 23, is a brand associate with Nike, part time artist, full time design hustler.
MARK BAJADE now lives in Upton Park E6.

GREEN SCENE #1
LONDON
FIELDS

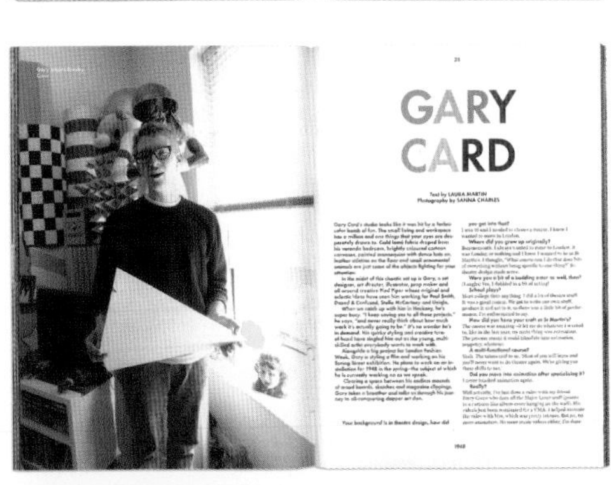
GARY
CARD

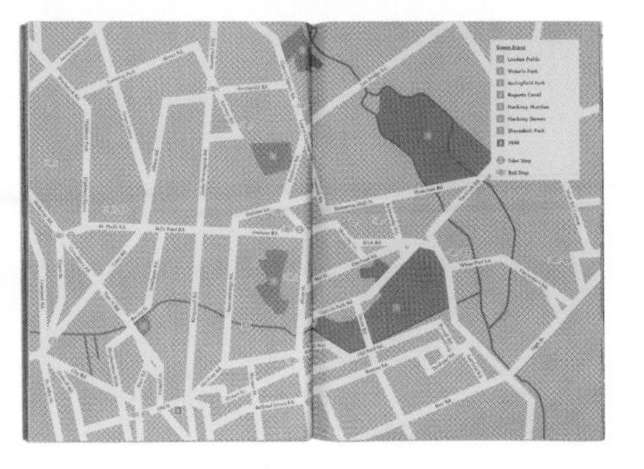

JEFF AWUAH, age 24, is a visionary.
JEFF AWUAH now lives in North London, N17.

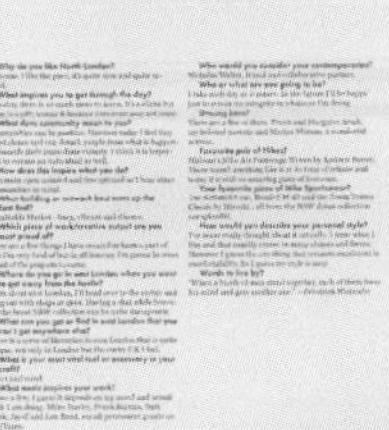

Typeface In Use
Futura ND

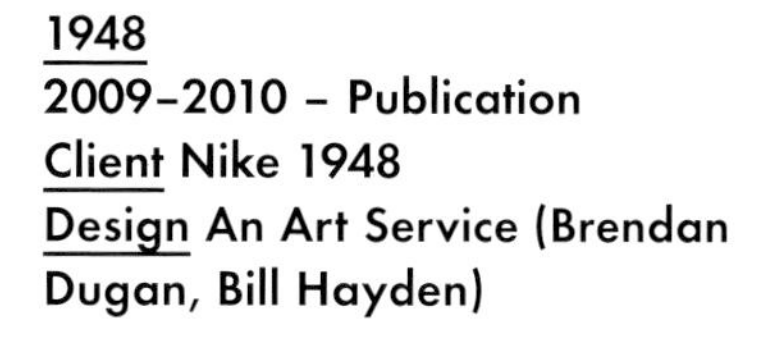
1948
2009–2010 – Publication
Client Nike 1948
Design An Art Service (Brendan Dugan, Bill Hayden)

1948 magazine documents the cultural landscape of East London, focusing on the artistic community involved with the 1948 Nike Sportswear boutique. A mix of portraits, interviews and vintage product appears alongside the neighborhood streets, parks and shops. Each issue uses distinct pop color combinations and overprinting of photography. Futura is employed as the main typeface for masthead, headlines and body copy, as a nod to Nike's design heritage—JUST DO IT.

"We intiallly thought Futura would be fun to use as a reference to the Nike heritage... JUST DO IT. Famously used extra bold condensed."

Typeface In Use
Futura Std Bold

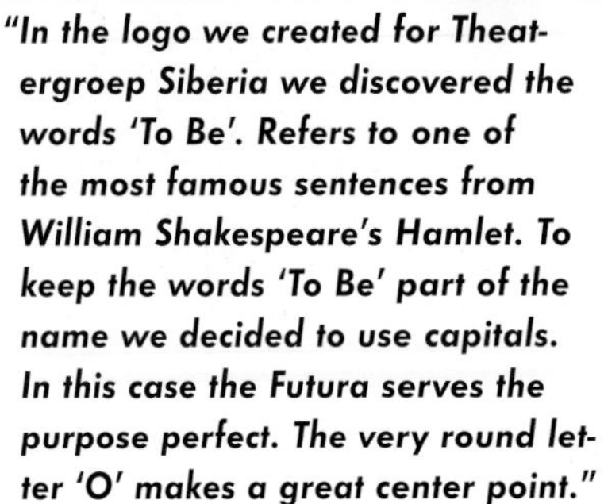

"In the logo we created for Theatergroep Siberia we discovered the words 'To Be'. Refers to one of the most famous sentences from William Shakespeare's Hamlet. To keep the words 'To Be' part of the name we decided to use capitals. In this case the Futura serves the purpose perfect. The very round letter 'O' makes a great center point."

O

almost Modern's Favorite Futura Letter Is 'O'.

It's a Man's World
2009 – Poster for a play
Client Theatergroep Siberia, Rotterdam, Netherlands
Design almost Modern

An A1 poster for the play *It's a man's world.*

Why Does Mrs. K Dress that Way?

2010 – T-shirt
Client Part of It (www.partofit.org)
Design Julian Bittiner

Typeface In Use
Architype Renner
(precursor to Futura)

I was invited by the non-profit initiative *Part of It* to design a T-shirt in support of a charity of my choice, with the sales of the T-shirt benefiting that charity (in this case *Dress for Success*). My design stems from my interest in the T-shirt as a medium and cultural icon. The text comes from a 1960s print advertisement that Marshall McLuhan references in *Understanding Media*. Mrs. K refers to then Soviet Premier Nikita Khrushchev's wife, Nina Khrushchev, and her habit of wearing simple, inexpensive clothing to emphasize her solidarity with ordinary Russians. This T-shirt prompts the viewer to consider the political implications of how you dress.

"The quote in the T-shirt references the Soviet Union and initially I looked for typefaces that were used in Russia around that time. However none of the typefaces I found felt right so I decided to be less literal and look for a typeface that evoked Soviet themes of egalitarianism, secularism, modernity, and revolution. Futura was radically modern in its day (particularly the experimental early drawings made by Paul Renner) and I felt it embodied these ideas well. The Soviet Union should have used it more."

Julian Bittiner's
Favorite Futura Letter
Is 'a'.

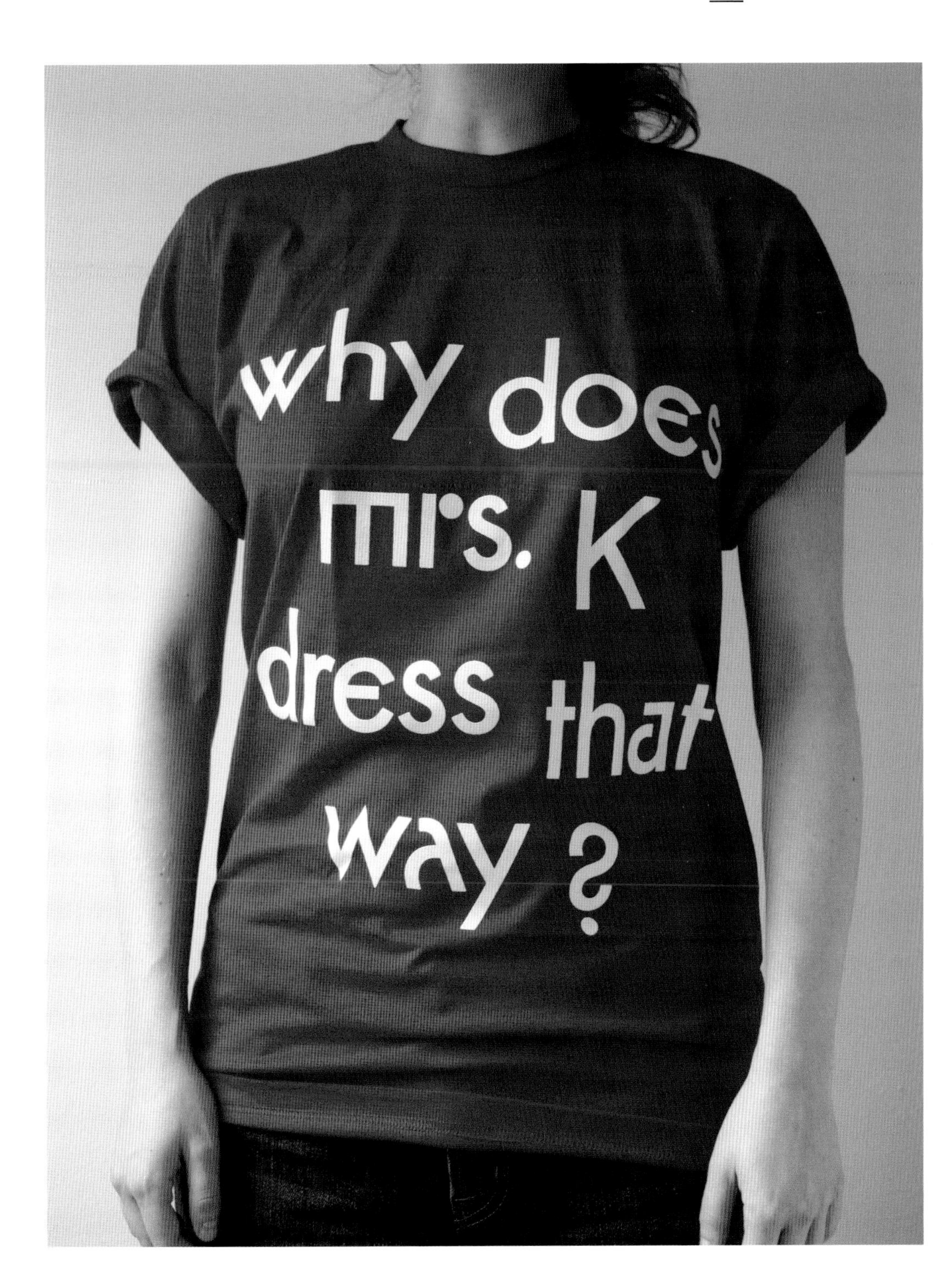
why does
mrs. K
dress that
way ?

"Futura is a geometric sans, yet it's not strictly geometric—there's a tension in the face between logic and visual judgment. It also seemed like a natural choice since the letters in 'LOGIC' are composed entirely of verticals, horizontals, and circles."

Typeface In Use
Futura, Bendigo, Braggadocio

Your Own/Another Logic
2008 – Poster
Design Neil Donnelly

"To feel your own logic clash with another logic, to be suddenly drawn into another rhythm, another rationality, a different set of rules: it's a profound experience, causing you to see the world with different eyes." This quote from an interview with Experimental Jetset provided the inspiration for a series of posters, an iterative project that involved working and re-working ideas, using forms created in one version as source material for the next. At times, I abandoned any sort of strict logic altogether in an effort to work more intuitively, to explore the relationship between arbitrariness and order.

G

Neil Donnelly's
Favorite Futura Letter
Is 'G'.

"The font the Van Abbemuseum, Eindhoven used in its previous logo was very geometrically based. The font Toekomst—based on the Futura—relates to this logo but is more defined. In the current Van Abbe logo some of the characters are referring to the previous logo ('A' 'U' 'M'). The current logo: Besides the Futura, Toekomst is also used in several works of art (for example the works of Barbara Kruger). Because of that it has an 'art-ish' touch."

Van Abbemuseum, Eindhoven
2008 – Identity
Client Van Abbemuseum, Eindhoven
Design 75B

The concept is based on the previous Van Abbemuseum identity. The museum used to have a logotype based on a mathematical system. 75B did keep some elements of the old logotype. And added a font named Toekomst, which is based on the Futura font. (Toekomst means "future" in dutch). Futura is also based on a geometrical system.
So it suited quite well. It was also chosen because it has an artistic touch. Several sub-identities were made since the identity exists. *Heartand, Trio exhibition, PLAY Van Abbe.* They all include the font Toekomst though.

Typeface In Use
Futura, Toekomst

Dan Peterman
Peter Guralnick
Peter Friedl
Marjetica Potrč
Wilhelm Sasnal
Ernesto Pujol
Deb Sokolow
Clare & the Reasons
Scott Hocking

JUTTA KOETHER
JO BAER
LYNDA BENGLIS
OUDBOUW

Plug In
to PLAY
vanabbemuseum

CINEMA, FOR US, IS THE MOST IMPORTANT OF THE ARTS
CINEMA ABOUT FOR ME ?
Plug In
to PLAY
vanabbemuseum

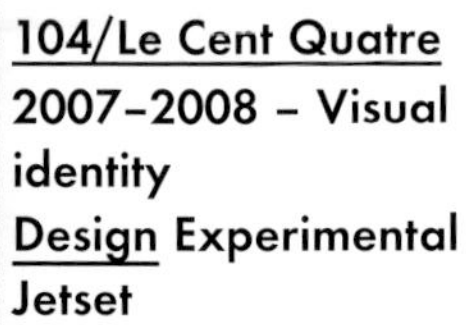

104/Le Cent Quatre
2007–2008 – Visual identity
Design Experimental Jetset

In the beginning of 2007, we were invited by a group of French curators to visit them in Paris. We met them in a very large construction pit, an enormous empty hall, measuring almost 36.000 square meters. This hall was to become the location of 104 (Le Cent Quatre), a new French cultural institute that would open its doors in October 2008. Situated in the 19th arrondissement, 104 is a very ambitious project, housing several exhibition spaces, theater halls, concert venues, stores, and apartments for artists-in-residence.

To make a long story short, the curators asked us to develop their graphic identity and sign system. Or to be more precise: they asked us to design a graphic manual, a "charte graphique", for other designers to work with. It was a very complicated construction: because of all kinds of reasons (legal, political, bureaucratic and cultural reasons), we were only allowed to work on the graphic manual, while other design studios would then be responsible for applying this manual to all the different parts of the graphic identity (sign system, website, etc.).

It was an awkward construction, especially for us. In our way of working, we put a lot of emphasis on the finished, designed object; we really believe in producing actual, physical artifacts. To shift our focus from making objects to creating instructions was not easy for us. In fact, it proved to be impossible, and this whole situation turned out to be one of the reasons of our break-up with Le Cent Quatre in 2008.

But let's not move ahead here, and return to the beginning of 2007. Although we realized it would be a difficult bureaucratic project, we still decided to accept the assignment. Even though we knew it could turn into a total failure, we still thought it was exciting to be involved.

During our first meeting, we noticed that one of the curators' main themes, program-wise, was the concept of the "work-in-progress": the idea that 104, as a project, is never finished, always evolving, eternally "under construction". So our starting point was to search for a sign system that would refer to the concept of the "work-in-progress". That's when we became interested in the concept of scaffolding.

A scaffold (in French, "échafaudage", in Dutch "stellage" or "steiger") is a structure that automatically refers to "work-in-progress"; it is immediately associated with construction sites, and the activity of building in general. We realized that a sign system based on the idea of scaffolding would be a constant reminder of the continuous cycle of building, demolishing and rebuilding. An échafaudage also has a very natural appearance. It has the casualness of a "ready-made" object; it will fit in the building in a completely natural way.

What we also found interesting about échafaudages is the concept of the iron construction. In Walter Benjamin's "The Arcades Project" a whole chapter is dedicated to the history and ideology of metal constructions, and the use of iron in winter gardens, railroad stations, the

Eiffel Tower, but especially the use of iron in passages and arcades. And the building of Le Cent Quatre really is an arcade, a passage. It is a street with a roof, built towards the end of the 19th century.

We already knew Walter Benjamin wrote a lot about this subject, so when we got involved in the project, one of the first things we did was studying his book "The Arcades Project", looking for clues and starting points. The fact that he wrote so much about iron constructions reinforced our idea to do something with échafaudages. By using iron constructions for the sign system of 104 (in the form of échafaudages), we hoped to emphasize the early-industrial architecture of Le Cent Quatre.

Another influence was the idea of the "street as a theater", or the "theater as a street", as expressed in the Constructivist stage designs (decors) of Liubov (Lyubov) Popova.

In short, the more we worked on it, the more we were convinced of the idea of using scaffolding structures as a sign system. Our plan was to create a sort of modular system of street furniture, a family of abstract forms referring to billboards, benches, traffic signs, pavilions and kiosks.

So basically, our idea was that these échafaudages would reinforce the idea of Le Cent Quatre as a street in itself, a fully functional street. By placing street furniture in there, or better said a sign system referring to street furniture, Le Cent Quatre would become a street, or a model of a street. At least, that was our plan.

Regarding the logo: it is interesting, when we first talked with the curators, they said

to us that they didn't want to have a logo. They were coming from a more postmodern, French way of thinking, and they thought that a logo would be too fixed, too static. So originally, we designed the logo just for ourselves, to have some material to sketch with. We slipped in some ideas for logos in our sketches for the sign system, but we actually expected that these logos would be voted off. Luckily, the curators loved the logos, so these logos ended up becoming an important part of the graphic identity.

The logo consists of three elements: a line, a circle, and a triangle. Together, these three elements form a stylized "104". We really like the idea of these geometric forms as "building blocks", as "bricks". We eventually developed a full logo system, in different weights, and also versions containing the text in full: "Le Cent Quatre".

What we also liked about the 104 logo is the fact that the line, the circle and the triangle very much refer to the idea of moving in space, of walking through a street. The stripe can be used as a line to be followed, the circle can be used as a spot to mark a location, and the triangle can be turned into an arrow. So the logo already contains, in itself, a miniature sign system.

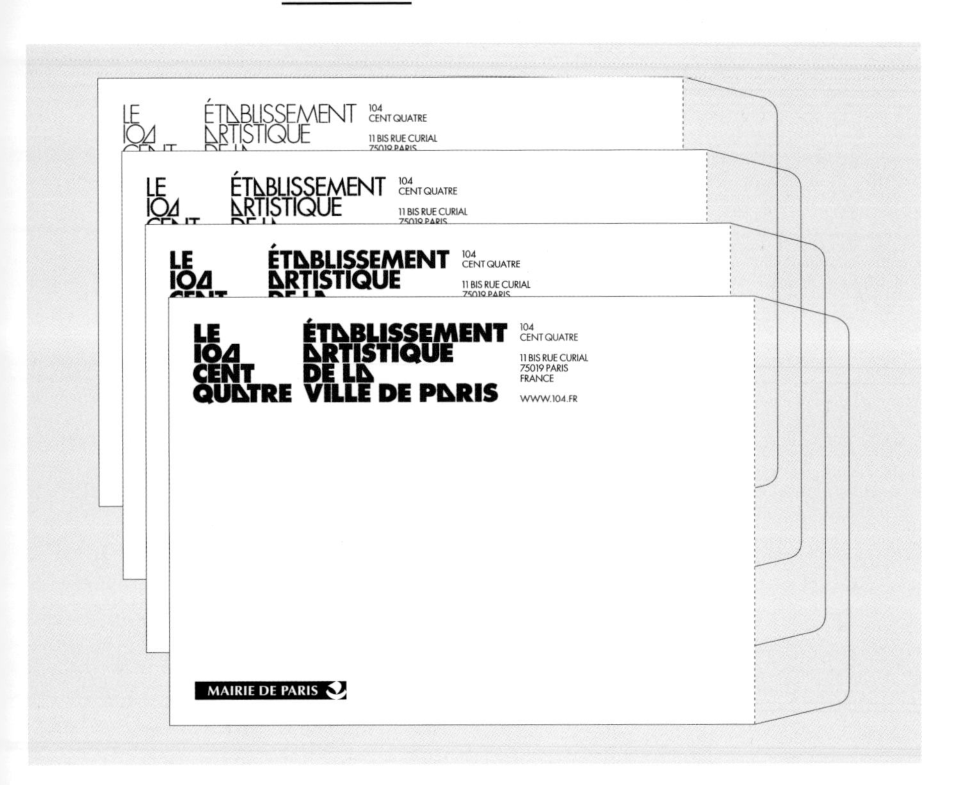

The typeface we used, in the 104 graphic identity as a whole, is Futura. As can be seen below, we replaced, in the standard Futura alphabet, both the letter "A" and number "4" for a triangle, and the number "0" for a round "O", to sort of reinforce the link between the logo and the typeface.

There are several reasons why we went for Futura. First of all, Futura is a geometric typeface, so it fits very well with the logo. And secondly, it's a typical early-industrial typeface, referring very much to the transition from the 19th century to the 20th century. So in that sense, it works very well within the context of a passage, an arcade. (True, Futura is a German typeface. But we think that the fact that Futura is a German typeface doesn't necessarily have to be problematic in a French context. In fact, there is a certain parallel to be drawn between Futura in the context of 104, and Walter Benjamin in the Parisian passages. Both are German outsiders from the beginning of the 20th century, placed in the context of Paris in the late 19th century).

It's funny: after we decided to use Futura, we were walking around in Paris, and noticed that an overwhelming amount of Parisian stores (hairdressers, laundrettes etc.)

use Futura in their signs. We thought it was brilliant; we realized that using Futura in the context of 104 would really emphasize this whole idea of Le Cent Quatre as a model of a street.

As we already explained, what made this an unusual (and uneasy) assignment for us was the fact that we weren't allowed to design everything ourselves. From the start, the plan was that we would be creating an underlying graphic identity, for other designers to work with. However, once in a while, there were some lucky opportunities for us to design some actual printed matter for Le Cent Quatre.

Working on Le Cent Quatre kept us occupied for the better part of 2007, and also for the first half of 2008. We would

like to thank Frédéric Fisbach, Robert Cantarella and Constance de Corbière for inviting us, Naïa Sore and Cécile Renault for their ongoing support, and everybody else at 104 for collaborating with us.

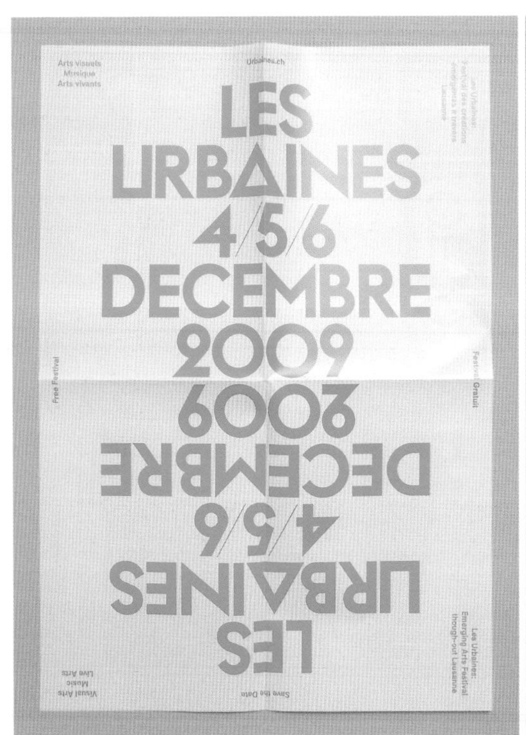
Arts visuels
Musique
Arts vivants
Urbaines.ch
LES
URBAINES
4/5/6
DECEMBRE
2009
Free Festival
Festival Gratuit
Save the Date
Visual Arts
Music
Live Arts
Les Urbaines:
Emerging Arts Festival
though-out Lausanne

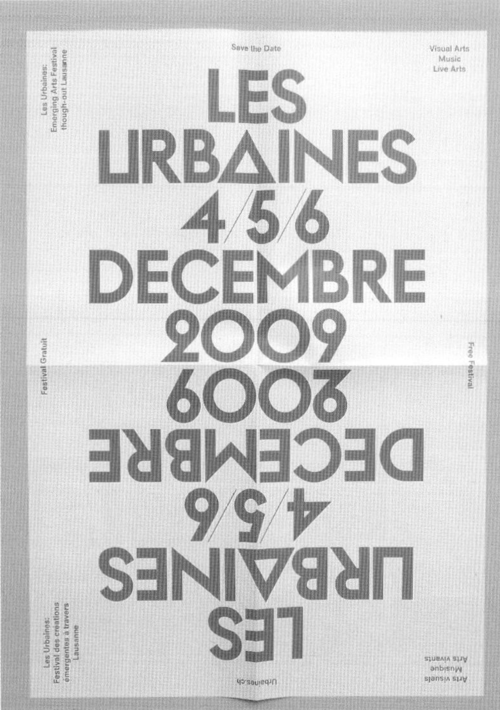
Save the Date
Visual Arts
Music
Live Arts
Les Urbaines:
Emerging Arts Festival
though-out Lausanne
LES
URBAINES
4/5/6
DECEMBRE
2009
Festival Gratuit
Free Festival
Les Urbaines:
Festival des créations
émergentes à travers
Lausanne
Urbaines.ch
Arts visuels
Musique
Arts vivants

Les Urbaines:
Festival des créations
émergentes à travers
Lausanne
Free Festival
Gratuit
Les Urbaines:
Emerging Arts Festival
though-out Lausanne
Save the Date
Visual Arts
Music
Live Arts

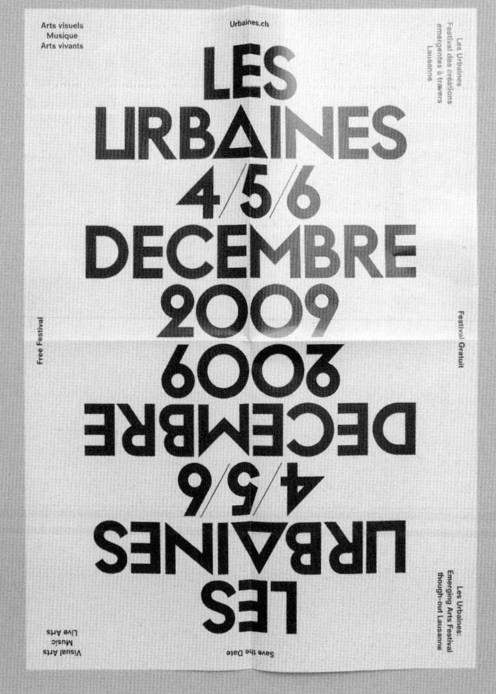
Arts visuels
Musique
Arts vivants
Urbaines.ch
Les Urbaines
Festival des créations
émergentes à travers
Lausanne
LES
URBAINES
4/5/6
DECEMBRE
2009
Free Festival
Festival Gratuit
Les Urbaines:
Emerging Arts Festival
though-out Lausanne
Save the Date
Visual Arts
Music
Live Arts

Les Urbaines
2009 – Custom typeface design for festival identity
Client Les Urbaines: Emerging Arts Festival, Lausanne, Switzerland
Type design Emmanuel Rey
Layout Jonathan Hares, Philippe Egger

Euclid is a geometric and constructed typeface. It was originally designed for *Les Urbaines*, and will be soon released as a complete font family. The brief was to design a typeface that produces the power of a logotype. The solution was to draw an easy identifiable set of numbers and alternates based on the triangle, square and circle.

Typeface In Use
Euclid (custom typeface)

"Using text as a logotype."

2

Emmanuel Rey's Favorite Futura Number Is '2'.

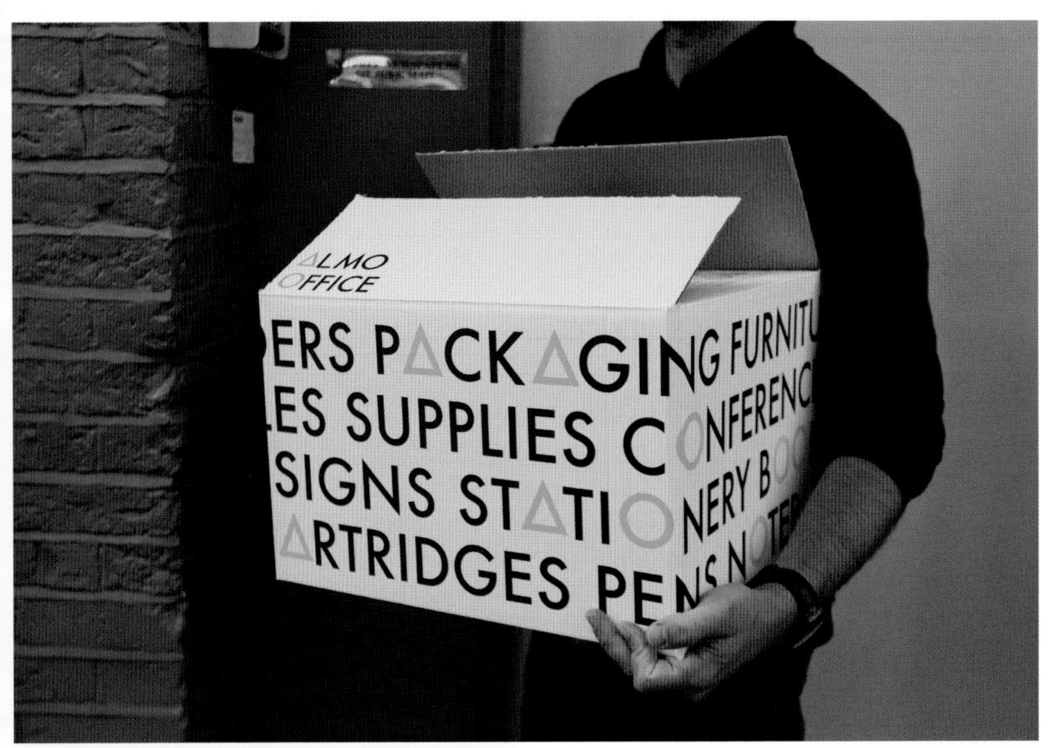

Typeface In Use
Futura

"Classic, simple typeface which could be developed for use with triangle and circle."

Almo Rebrand
2009 – Corporate identity
Client Almo Office
Design Company (Alex Swain)

Based on their original "triangular" logo, we developed the identity by abstracting the company's initials, "A" and "O", into a simpler geometric form. We then created a recurring motif which reinforces brand recognition. The green and black color scheme was chosen to reflect the company's carbon-neutral credentials, underlined by the use of recycled paper throughout all applications. It's a circle!

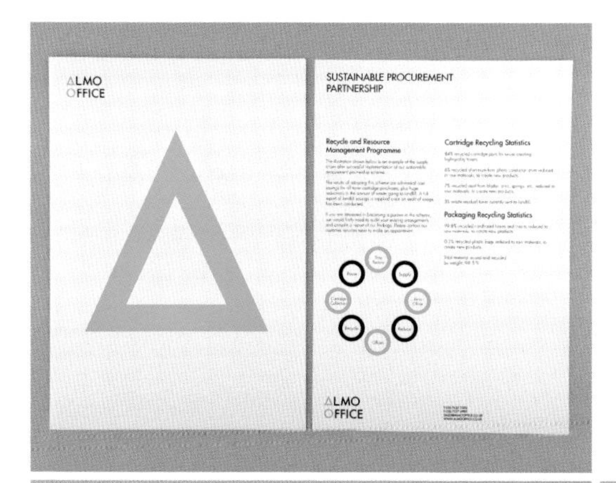

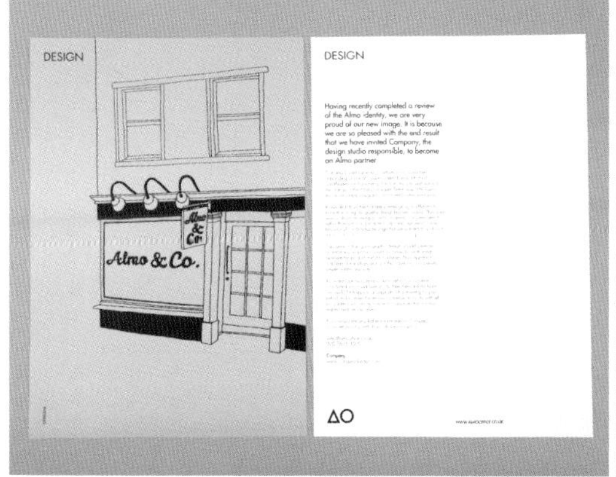

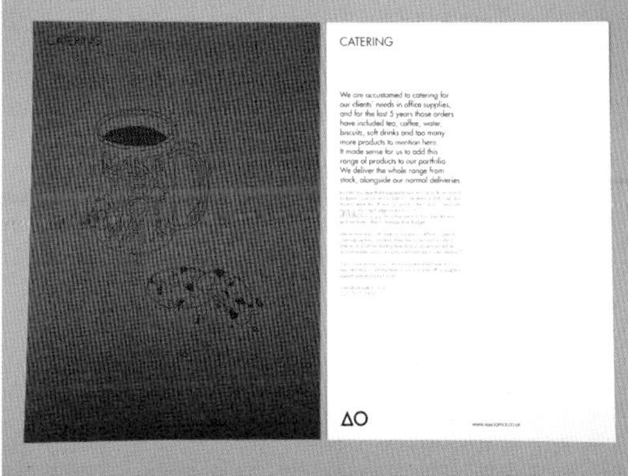

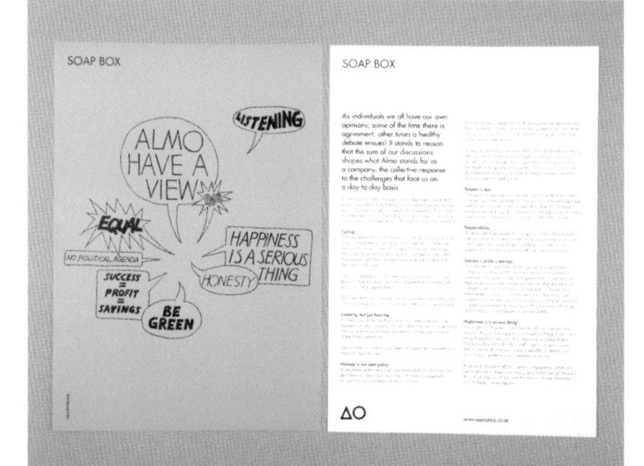

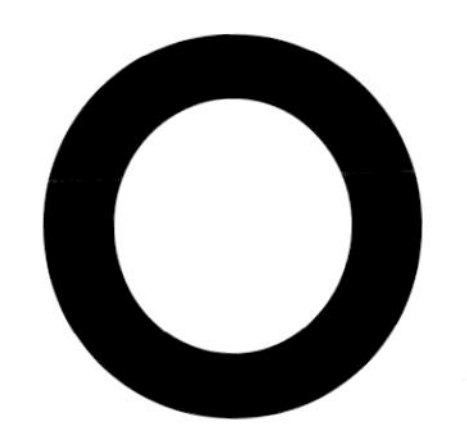

Alex Swain's Favorite Futura Letter Is 'O'.

Standard 8
2008 – Identity and literature
Client Standard 8
Design Browns (Creative direction - Nick Jones, Design - Stephen McGilvray)

Typeface In Use
Futura

Standard 8 specialize in designing and manufacturing three dimensional objects—everything from one-off tables to universal exhibition systems. In a reflection of the company's product and design, *Standard 8*'s identity is anything but standard: it is made up of eight different logos each made up of eight figure 8s from eight typefaces. The idea is that you take an easily recognizable form like a figure eight and create something interesting and beautiful in its own right. We found out later that the flower-like symbols are called "fluerons". Each piece of stationery uses a different flueron. The letterhead is foil blocked using a flourescent orange foil, the continuation is debossed. The business cards and compliment cards have a full set of the logos foil blocked onto the reverse, again in flourescent orange. The eight logos are accompanied by a simple wordmark.

"Modernist, clean and symmetrical"

8

Browns' Favorite
Futura Number Is '8'.

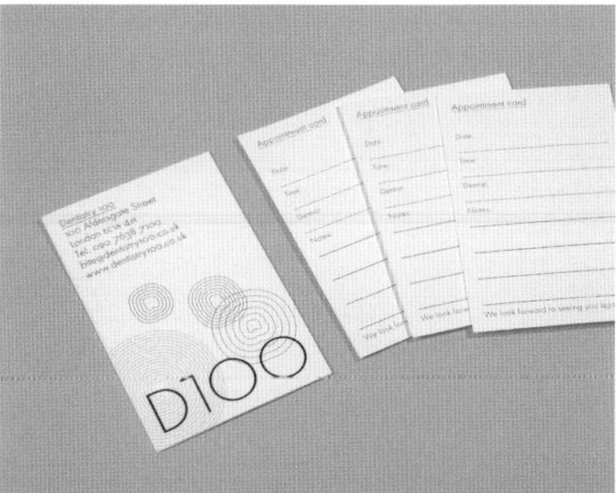

Typeface In Use
Futura ND Light

D100 Idenity
2009 – Idenity
Client D100 Dentistry
Design Mind Design (Creative direction - Holger Jacobs, Art direction - Craig Sinnamon)

D100 is a modern dentistry at the Barbican (100 Aldersgate street). The identity is inspired by the raking patterns around stones in Japanese Zen gardens and protective layers of enamel around teeth. The pattern have also been applied to the interior going around furniture and various fixed or removable object in the practice.

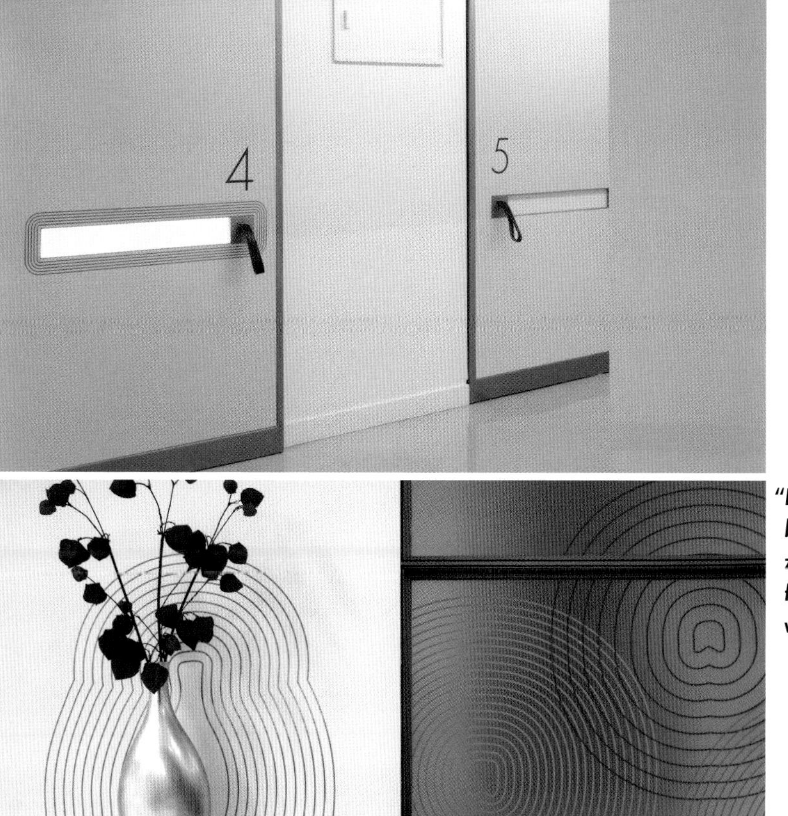

"Futura was used because it has a round zero in the old style figures which worked well with the logo."

HAPPY?
2007 – Poster, flyer
Client Fabrica | The Benetton group communications research center
Design Dominic Prevost

These posters/flyers were used to promote a Fabrica sponsored event questioning happiness and its components. By using a vectorized illustration treatment, I tried to break away as far as possible from an emotive, photographic or illustrative treatment, instead relying on quotes regarding happiness seamlessly intertwined with the illustrations, to give it depth and character. Quotes are all about the "wrong" things that grand us happiness, may it be drugs, plastic surgery, or manscaping, don't you hate manscaping? This project was created at Fabrica, 2007.

Typeface In Use
Futura

R

Dominic Prevost's Favorite Futura Letter Is 'R'.

75B
www.75b.nl

75B come up with ideas for themselves and for others. They get something in their heads and wish to translate that into a visible form so others may see it too. This translation process also leads to new things that may sometimes look like copies of "ordinary" things and then again take the form of self-referential abstractions. And that is why, in this society that is already overflowing with stuff, these designers contribute to the production of even more goods, stuff, objects, things, and printed matter. Although it is actually about something immaterial: the idea. In a studio in Rotterdam people are constantly working on ideas, under the supervision of Pieter Vos and Rens Muis. When these ideas are realized they bear the signature "75B". Whether this production will ever cease is hard to predict, even by the designers themselves.
–pp. 136–139

Ahonen & Lamberg
www.ahonenandlamberg.com

Ahonen & Lamberg is a multi-disciplinary design studio based in Paris. Founded in 2006 by Anna Ahonen and Katariina Lamberg, it covers a wide range of areas and an equally vast client list ranging from multinational companies or luxury brands to emerging artists. The aim of the studio is to translate each client's particular universe through any media, be it print, product or even environment. The Ahonen & Lamberg design principal is to balance classical and alternative design, creating a tone that is always elegant, recognizable and yet eager to surprise. Contrasts and challenges are key to the work. Anna and Katariina are also co-founders and art directors of the magazine Dossier.
–p. 125

almost Modern
www.almostmodern.com

A graphic design studio consisting of a graphic designer (Jorn de Vries) and an artist (Markus Rummens). This vivid combination reflects in the work.
–pp. 130–131

An Art Service
www.anartservice.com

An Art Service is a graphic design and art direction company located in New York City, working in publications, branding and websites.
–pp. 128–129

Axel Peemoeller
www.axelpeemoeller.com

Axel Peemoeller, graphic designer, 33, living/working in Hamburg, Germany and Barcelona, Spain. Studied visual communication in Düsseldorf, Hamburg and Melbourne. Axel has been working for clients and studios as a freelance contractor, as designer, senior designer and project manager for the last 13 years. He has developed and designed corporate identities, magazines, books, typefaces, photographical imagery, visual interfaces and environmental design for large international and small boutique clients all the around the world. His design is concept-driven, edgy and with an inventive touch, underlined by his creative and outside-the-box thinking. He draws inspiration from life in general, nature and science.
–p. 62–63

Big Active
www.bigactive.com

Big Active is a D&AD award winning creative consultancy specializing in art direction, graphic design and the representation of leading image-makers. Big Active believes in creative networks—its aim is to produce creative design and commercial art based upon ideas with an accessible common touch.
–p. 115

Bisdixit
www.bisdixit.com

Bis was founded in 1996 by Alex Gifreu (Maó, 1971) and Pere Alvaro (Palafrugell, 1967). Bis' crew is made by the young talent of Carles Murillo, Sara Santos and Ana Domínguez as senior designers and Carme Lopez as office manager. The studio is based in Barcelona and Figueres.The company's work is focused in the cultural industry, developing projects for a number of renowned public and private institutions in Spain and abroad. Bis has been distinguished with several national design prizes such as Laus, Anuaria, Visual and also international ones as The One Show, Tokyo Type Directors Club and Art Director's Club. Their work has been published in different books and magazines including Visual, Eye, Emigre, Tipográfica, Novum, etc.
–p. 61

Browns
www.brownsdesign.com

Browns is a creative consultancy with an international reputation for elegant, powerful and distinctive communications. Our work spans identity, literature, digital, editorial, financial reporting and events. We are independent. No links, no tie-ups, no distractions. All our energies go into looking after our clients. We don't like saying no, so please don't ask us to free-pitch or work for unethical causes. Challenging briefs bring out the best in us—there is no design without discovery. You know more about your business than we do, so be prepared for lots of tricky questions. Sometimes we might take your customer's side, but good design always puts its audience first. The best solutions do more than give answers; they open new possibilities. When delivered with originality, beauty and intelligence, they move organizations forward. This is what Browns does. And it's why clients of all shapes and sizes, such as Invesco, Channel 4, BAFTA, Hiscox and Dries Van Noten believe in us.
–pp. 150–151

Bureau Mirko Borsche
www.mirkoborsche.com

Bureau Mirko Borsche is a Munich based graphic design studio founded by Mirko Borsche in 2007. The studio has been producing numerous projects such as magazines, catalogues, books, posters, typefaces, identities, industrial design, fashion design, exhibition design, movies and websites. Our clients hail from the fields of culture and business.
–pp. 102–103

BVD
www.bvd.se

BVD is a design and branding agency specialized in every physical touchpoint of a brand, in and around a retail environment. Our approach is based on a combination of consumer insight, business focus, ideas and design. We view design as a strategic marketing tool. As such, it's primary role is to communicate the brand in a relevant way—and to deliver concrete and measurable results. BVD was founded in 1997 by Catrin Vagnemark and Carin Blidholm. Today, it has four partners and some 25 employees. Clients include global Swedish consumer brands as well as companies from the USA, Japan, Norway and Germany.
–pp. 64–65

Byggstudio
www.byggstudio.com

Byggstudio is a young design consultancy developing visual communication and strategic concepts. Byggstudio was founded in 2006 by Hanna Nilsson, Sofia Østerhus and Markus Bergström after MA graduation in visual communication and product design from Danmarks Designskole in Copenhagen and Royal College of Art in London.
–pp. 10–13

C100 Purple Haze
www.c100purplehaze.com

C100 Purple Haze is a Munich based multi-disciplinary design consultancy founded by Christian Hundertmark (C100) and Clemens Baldermann (Purple Haze). The studio's diverse output included projects for miscellaneous public and private clients on a variety of national and international projects including expertise in conception, art direction, typography, design and illustration. Specialized in delivering inventive and precise visual solutions we approach each project with enthusiasm, dedicated hands, and an individual style which is evident in our works.
–pp. 20–21

Company/Alex Swain
www.company-london.com

Company is a design consultancy. We develop brand identities, publications and websites. As our name suggests, we like working in the company of others. Our designs are inspired by a desire to make people think, smile or see things differently.
–pp. 148–149

Dani Navarro & Bendita Gloria
www.daninavarro.com
www.benditagloria.com

Dani Navarro is a graphic design studio based in Barcelona.
Bendita Gloria is a graphic design studio focused on print design and based in Barcelona.
–pp. 36–37

Daniel Carlsten
www.danielcarlsten.com

After having spent several years as an art director, graphic designer and illustrator at the creative collective Acne, I decided to launch my own business. My main interest and expertise lie in visual identities and graphic design of printed matter such as books, catalogues, stationeries, posters, invitations and packaging.
–p. 39

Dominic Prevost
www.dominicprevost.com

A tall skinny guy with a weird nose and a love for RGB images that always come out wrong in the CMYK printer. (I guess I'll never learn).
–pp. 154–155

Emmanuel Rey
www.emmanuelrey.ch

Freelance and self-employed type and graphic designer, currently working in Berlin and in Switzerland.
–pp. 146–147

Everything Design
www.everythingdesign.co.nz

Everything are a New Zealand based graphic design company with a no nonsense approach to brand strategy and brand identity design, brand guidelines, brochures, websites, marketing communications, vehicle liveries, destination branding, exhibition design, signage, clothing and uniforms, advertising campaigns, marketing suites, annual reports, logos, information graphics, e-newsletters, posters, direct mail, furniture, bikes, packaging, games... Everything.
–p. 114

Experimental Jetset
www.experimentaljetset.com

We are Experimental Jetset, a small, independent graphic design studio based in Amsterdam, consisting of three persons: Marieke Stolk, Danny van den Dungen and Erwin Brinkers. We have been collaborating as Experimental Jetset since we graduated from the Gerrit Rietveld Academy (in 1997, 1997 and 1998 respectively), and in our work we focus mostly on printed matter.
–pp. 108–111, 140–145

Felix Müthe
www.felixmuethe.com

1983 Born in Ulm, Germany 2006–10 Visual Communications at Pforzheim University (BA) 09/08–03/09 Internship at Bureau Mirko Borsche, Munich
–p. 105

Filip Matejícek
www.pestrographique.com

I'm Filip, I'm currently studying graphic design at the Pilsen College of Art and Design.
My work featured is a combination of self-initiated projects, freelance work as well as works done at school.
–pp. 122–123

Gloor & Jandl
www.g-j.ch

Hannes Gloor (1982), Designer
Stefan Jandl (1983), Designer
We are a small, independent graphic design studio based in Zurich, Switzerland. Our work mainly consists of printed matter such as books, magazines and posters. It also includes logotypes, corporate identities and photography. We work on client commissions as well as on self-initiated projects.
–pp. 48–51, 104

Henrik Nygren Design
www.henriknygrendesign.se

Henrik Nygren Design mainly deals with analyzing the client's market potential, with strategy in accordance with this potential and the design and production of books, magazines, packaging, corporate identities, advertising campaigns, exhibitions, etc. When necessary, and depending on the nature of the assignment, the company enlists a carefully selected group of brand strategists, copywriters, printers, etc. Clients turn to us to obtain the greatest possible quality from given circumstances. When possible, we meet all expectations. Every now and then, we surpass them.
–pp. 26–35

Hi/Megi Zumstein & Claudio Barandun
www.hi-web.ch

Hi was founded in 2007 by Megi Zumstein and Claudio Barandun. We are mainly working inbook design, poster design and signage systems. Megi (1973), studied Visual Communication at the University of Art &Design in Zurich (HGKZ). Since 2004 she teaches at the University of Applied Sciences Art & Design in Lucerne (HSLU) in the field of Graphic Design. She has participated in exhibitions in Zurich (CH), Sarnen (CH), Paris (FR), Tehran (IR), Ingolstadt (DE).
Claudio Barandun, (1979), studied Graphic design at the University of Art & Design in Lucerne. He is co-editor of the Comic-magazine "Strapazin" (www.strapazin.ch). Since 2008 he is teaching graphic design and photography at Neue Schule für Gestaltung Langenthal. Some of Claudios posters have been awarded (100-best-posters in Germany, Austria and Switzerland, ADC prize Switzerland and Poster-Biennial in Tehran).
–pp. 77, 81, 86–87, 90

Hype Type Studio
Paul Hutchison
www.hypetype.co.uk

Formed in 1999 by Paul Hutchison, Hype Type is a multi-disciplinary graphic design and communications studio with over ten years experience working closely with local, national and international clients. We have built a reputation for producing relevant, memorable and effective creative solutions. Our experience extends across many areas including the arts, leisure, consumer goods and services, government, healthcare, media and entertainment, youth culture, technology, retail, music and fashion industries.
–pp. 82–83

Joe Hinder
www.joehinder.co.uk

A graduate from Bath Spa University. Keen to provoke change and encourage new thinking, interested in bringing visuals to information and sound.
–pp. 52–53

Jonas Hegi
www.jonashegi.com

My name is Jonas Hegi. I'm a student of the Zurich University of the Arts, Switzerland. I live and work in Zurich.
–pp. 18–19

Julian Bittiner
www.appliedaesthetics.org

Julian Bittiner is an independent designer based in Queens, New York, and a lecturer in graphic design at Yale University School of Art. Originally from Geneva, Switzerland, he studied fine art and graphic design at Art Center College of Design, subsequently receiving an MFA in graphic design from Yale in 2008. His practice is situated primarily within the cultural sector and is characterized by an interest in the shared histories of fine and applied arts, and their evolving relationship with the public realm.
–pp. 132–133

Klein
www.carstenklein.com

Klein is an international graphic design consultancy, launched in London in 2002, now based in Amsterdam. With clients in the UK, Netherlands, Germany and the U.S., it specializes in visual communication and brand identities with a strong focus on printed matter and typography, as well as websites.
–pp. 88–89, 94–95

KIDNAP YOUR DESIGNER
www.kidnapyourdesigner.com

K.Y.D. is Caroline Dath + Damien Safie + guests.
Kidnap Your Designer is the name of a Belgian graphic design agency created in 2006 by Caroline Dath, graduated from Saint-Luc Liège and from ERG (Graphic Research School). Damien Safie, a classmate from ERG, joined her in 2008. The studio, based in Brussels, produces creative works with the use of typography and printing techniques for clients from the music, theater, cinema, design or architecture fields.Kidnap Your Designer also creates experimental video projects and self-produced projects (postcards, A4-Fold your clothes, note,...).
For each project the studio develops its graphic design around an idea, a concept closely related to the subject involved. Graphic design should not exist without ideas. Sense makes graphicdesign then designgraphic makes sense. Caroline Dath teaches at ERG
(Ecole de Recherche Graphique) Brussels, in graphic design section. She also gave lessons at Ecole Supérieure des Arts Saint-Luc Liège in graphic design section in 2008.
–p. 60

Lesley Moore
Graphic Designers
www.lesley-moore.nl

Lesley Moore is an Amsterdam-based graphic design agency, founded in May 2004 by Karin van den Brandt (1975, Blerick, Netherlands) and Alex Clay (1974, Lørenskog, Norway). Van den Brandt and Clay studied at the Arnhem Academy of the Arts (Netherlands). Current and recent clients include: BIS publishers, Centraal Museum Utrecht, Mark Magazine, MTV, De Volkskrant (Gorilla, in collaboration with Herman van Bostelen and De Designpolitie), Warmoesmarkt, Wilfried Lentz Art Gallery, Wolters Kluwer. Merits include: European Design Awards for best Magazine 2008, Official selection Chaumont 2008, European Design Awards Miscellaneous and Jury Award 2007, Art Directors Club Netherlands 2007 and Dutch Design Awards 2007.
–pp. 69, 80

Make_Studio
www.makestudio.co.uk

We consist of a core of designers, directors, artists and creative thinkers with strong external links with our printers and photographers to provide an integrated network of interesting people. Using specialists within their field, we have also been able to adapt to needs of our clients and create a greater capacity for work whilst retaining overall project direction under the roof of Make_Studio.
-p. 124

Manifiesto Futura
www.manifiestofutura.com

Manifiesto Futura, an independent studio formed by Vicky González and Ivan Garcia aka Boronas. We love our work. We take responsibility of the results, because we're the ones who take care of every detail in our projects. We cherish experimentation, the value of the message sent and the intelligent provocation. We believe in function over form, celebrate clear content. We're Mexican.
-pp. 96–97

mfsworks
Mercè Fernández
Graphic Design and
Art Direction
www.mfsworks.com

Graduate of the Escuela Eina of Barcelona in graphic design, she has gained work experience in studios like Enric Aguilera Asociados and Cla-se. For the last two years she works as a freelance, developing projects on communication, publications and corporate identity.
-pp. 76, 78–79, 92

Mind Design
www.minddesign.co.uk

Mind Design is a London-based independent graphic design studio founded by Holger Jacobs in 1999 after graduating from the Royal College of Art. The studio specializes in the development of visual identities and has worked for a wide range of clients in different sectors.
-pp. 66–67, 74–75, 100–101, 152–153

-nada-
www.designbynada.com

-nada- is a Lisbon based graphic design studio. Founded in 2006, our work includes posters for exhibitions and theaters, corporate identities, book design, magazines, sleeve design, webdesign, illustration and motion graphics.
-pp. 120–121

Neil Donnelly
www.neildonnelly.net

Neil Donnelly is a graphic designer who makes printed matter, websites, and exhibitions, and occasionally videos and typefaces. He has worked with Yale University, Storefront for Art and Architecture, The New School, and the School of the Art Institute of Chicago, among others. He teaches graphic design at Rutgers University and holds an MFA from Yale.
-pp. 134–135

Neo Neo
www.neoneo.ch

Neo Neo is a graphic design studio founded by Xavier Erni and Thuy-An Hoang, in Geneva, Switzerland. We met at the Geneva University of Arts and Design in 2006. After both working as graphic designers in Paris in 2009, we came back in Geneva to open our own agency. We specially like working on printed matter for artistic or cultural projects. Designing books, magazines, visual identities or posters is what we prefer.
-pp. 56–57

Niels Schrader &
Eike Dingler
www.nielsschrader.de
www.minddesign.info
www.eikedingler.de

Niels Schrader is an Amsterdam-based graphic designer, born in 1977 in Caracas, Venezuela. He graduated in communication design at the University of Applied Sciences in Düsseldorf in 2003 and further completed his academic studies in the master programme at the Sandberg Institute Amsterdam. Before setting up his own studio in 2005, Schrader had worked as a freelance designer for Uwe Loesch and Irma Boom. His portfolio of clients includes the Graphic Design Museum Breda, the Mondriaan Foundation Amsterdam, the Leiden University Academy of Creative and Performing Arts, the Berlage Institute and KCAP Architects&Planners in Rotterdam. He currently teaches at the Willem de Kooning Academy in Rotterdam. Eike Dingler studied communication design in Düsseldorf, Germany and Arnhem, Netherlands. Funded by a DAAD-scholarship he graduated from the TypeMedia postgraduate course in Type Design and Typography at the Royal Academy of Fine Arts in The Hague in 2007. He then started his own studio. Currently he lives in Berlin.
-p. 126

Oliver Daxenbichler
www.oliverdaxenbichler.com

Oliver Daxenbichler, founder of Oliver Daxenbichler Design, Inc., is a 33 year old art director and graphic designer who lives and works currently in Frankfurt Main, Germany. Over the the course of almost one decade he has been working on a large variety of print and new media based projects including conceptualizing and producing ad campaigns and catalogues, logos and brand identities and magazine design.
-pp. 91, 106–107

Paulus M. Dreibholz
Atelier for Typography and
Graphic Design
www.dreibholz.com

Paulus M. Dreibholz is a typographer and graphic designer based in London. The output of his atelier reveals his focus on editorial and typographic design in the form of printed matter, corporate identities, typefaces and exhibition pieces. His studio work is continuously substantiated and challenged by his writing and teaching practice. Dreibholz' approach to design is based on his theory of the inherent meaning of form and the human understanding of it. Dreibholz is currently lecturer at the BA Graphic Design and MA Communication Design course at Central Saint Martins and at the University of Applied Arts Vienna. He regularly conducts typographic workshops and lectures at colleges and universities across Europe and is a founding member of TeachingType (www.teachingtype.com), a platform for exchange between educators in the field of visual communication. Dreibholz' work has won various awards and has been featured extensively in publications and exhibitions.
-pp. 118–119

Pot & van der Velden
graphic designers
www.potvandervelden.nl

Pot & van der Velden is a graphic design studio by Theo-Bert Pot and Isabel van der Velden. The studio is based in The Hague, Netherlands. We focus on the development of visual identities, posters and editorial design. Pot & van der Velden works from various market segments, commercial and cultural. Typography, concept and function are the three words where we start from with every single assignment.
-pp. 54–55, 58–59

Roanne Adams
www.roanneadams.com

Studio
Roanne Adams is a multidisciplinary design studio devoted to holistic branding that serves a range of fashion, art, and lifestyle clients. Led by award-winning creative director Roanne Adams, the studio offers design, image, and branding capabilities across a variety of mediums, from print to moving image. By thoughtfully distilling a client's inspirations, ideas, and motivations, Roanne Adams generates fresh, sincere, compelling brand messages that engage and resonate.
Roanne opened her design studio in TriBeCa in 2006 after being awarded New Visual Artist by PRINT magazine. Prior to this, she worked as a designer and art director at Wolff Olins. Roanne holds a BFA in Communication Design from Parsons School of Design.
-pp. 22–23

Robi Jõeleht
www.robjoe.com

Freelance designer and illustrator based in Tallinn, Estonia.
-pp. 112–113

Robin Snasen Rengård
www.snasen.no

Robin Snasen Rengård is a graphic designer and illustrator from Oslo, Norway.
-pp. 42–43

Shaz Madani
www.smadani.com

Shaz Madani was born in 1984 in Iran and now lives and works in London. Since graduating from LCC in 2008, she has been involved in various projects and freelance work. Shaz works in all areas of design, from typography and illustration to 3D installations.
Education:
2003–2004 Central Saint Martins College of Art
2004–2008 London College of Communication
-pp. 40–41, 72–73

Sort Design
www.sortdesign.co.uk

Sort Design is a Belfast based graphic design and branding studio founded in 2006, working with its clients to enhance their businesses

and communications through effective design. With clients large and small across the UK and Ireland, Sort provide a full range of design services including company naming, branding, corporate communications, website design, marketing materials, and exhibition design. Sort aim to build long-term relationships with its clients, helping them achieve their goals through market relevant, applied creativity.
–pp. 46–47

Stout/Kramer
www.stoutkramer.nl

Marco Stout and Evelyne Kramer have worked since 1999 under the name Stout/Kramer. The graphic design unit has a special interest in the position the graphic designer can take in the communication process. "We are trained as graphic designers. The profession is constantly changing and as we see it, can no longer be defined.
Our way of working distinguishes itself by being conscious of the position the designer can take in the process. We don't want to set ourselves up as merely designers of a message. We see ourselves as editors and directors of communication. As editor, the designer interprets the content and context of a message. As director, the designer is responsible for the appropriate means of communication."
–pp. 68, 116–117

Studio Astrid Stavro
www.astridstavro.com

Astrid Stavro set up her own Barcelona based studio upon graduating with distinction from The Royal College of Art in 2005. She has since worked for the Museo Nacional Centro de Arte Reina Sofía, the Miró Foundation, the Generalitat de Catalunya, the Design Hub Barcelona, the Palau de la Música, the Art Directors Club of Europe, the Institute of Contemporary Art and numerous publishing houses. She co-runs the publishing house Infolio, lectures internationally and teaches editorial design at IDEP. The studio's work has been featured extensively in the press and has been recognized with more than 70 awards in less than four years. Astrid writes for various journals including Grafik and Étapes.
–pp. 14–15, 84–85, 93

Studio Laucke
www.studio-laucke.com

The Amsterdam-based Studio Laucke is founded in 2000 by its owner Dirk Laucke and executes commissions in the fields of corporate- and book design. Its assignments are mostly related to art and culture. Studio Laucke is multiple awarded with among others the Best Dutch Books, The Dutch Design Prize, The Dutch Corporate Identity Award, The Art Directors Club NY, The 100 Best Posters/Germany, Good 50x70/Italy, The European Design Award.
–pp. 70–71

StudioSpass
Jaron Korvinus &
Daan Mens
www.studiospass.com

StudioSpass: "pure spass in design". StudioSpass is us: Jaron Korvinus & Daan Mens. Since April 2008, we run an office for visual communication in the heart of Rotterdam, Netherlands. We specialize in making campaigns and visual identities, both in print and in pixels. StudioSpass is evolving into an all-round design office. We avoid being trapped into corners and fixed formulae, and we really value Spass and passion in design. StudioSpass: "Appreciation to us is hearing from our clients that they recognize the Spass we have in our work."
–pp. 24–25

Thorbjørn Ankerstjerne
www.ankerstjerne.co.uk

Thorbjørn Ankerstjerne hails from Copenhagen, Denmark but has spent the last seven years living in London where he graduated in 2007 with a BA in Graphic Design from Central Saint Martins. Since then he has directed music videos, designed identities, art directed various fashion brands; packaging, invitations, web and video. In early 2009 he published the first issue of the bi-annual publication FILE Magazine in collaboration with Fabio Sebastianelli—being the editor and art director. Thorbjørn Ankerstjerne is the daily editor of FILE's website (www.file-magazine.com).
–p. 127

us (design studio)
www.usdesignstudio.co.uk

We are a multi-disciplinary graphic design studio called us.Our work covers brand identity and development, art direction, advertising, motion,printed literature and web. We believe that design should stem from good ideas no matter how big or small. In our studio we look to create work that excites, inspires and most importantly meets the needs of the client.
–pp. 44–45

Why Not Smile/Hoon Kim
www.whynotsmile.com

Why Not Smile is an independent graphic design workshop based in New York City. Hoon Kim (Jeong-Hoon Kim) established the workshop in 2009 after completing an MFA in graphic design at the Rhode Island School of Design (RISD) in the U.S. Why Not Smile focuses on design for art, architecture and cultural clients across various media: printed matter, branding, exhibition design, motion graphics, and websites. We were awarded for AIGA Best 50 Books, Brno International Graphic Design Bienniale, and TDC Typographic Excellence. We also participated in diverse exhibitions dealing with space and sound in New York, London, Lausanne, and Seoul. Our current research attempts to visualize soundscapes in the public sphere to the printed space, in order to bridge the gap between the personal space and the public space.
–p. 38

Trafik
www.lavitrinedetrafik.fr

Trafik is a creative studio consisting of graphic designers, typographers, computer programmers, digital animators and artists. Whether working on an institutional, commercial, or cultural project, Trafik seamlessly blends two approaches: conventional graphic design, and artistic experimentation. Trafik's collaboration with its diverse range of clients allows for an investigation into new technologies and the development of innovative concepts. Trafik affirms its vision through a series of visual and graphic experimentations, or with interactive artistic pieces which are conceived with audience participation in mind. These interactive works emphasize some of the key traits of the digital culture: usability, collectivity, exchange, and transmission. Trafik, with this unique approach, is regularly invited to exhibit work during artistic festivals and events.
–pp. 16–17

Xavier Barrade
www.xavierbarrade.com

23 year old freelance graphic designer, currently studying fine arts at Les Beaux Arts de Paris.
–pp. 98–99

Published and distributed by
viction:workshop ltd.

viction:ary™

Unit C, 7th Floor, Seabright Plaza,
9-23 Shell Street, North Point, Hong Kong
URL: www.victionary.com
Email: we@victionary.com

Edited & Designed by TwoPoints.Net
— The TwoPoints.Net team that worked on this book:
Martin Lorenz, Lupi Asensio, David Nagel,
Kosmas Sidiropoulos, Raby-Florence Fofana,
Felix Auer and Áxel Durana

Fonts in I Love Futura:
Futura ND Demi, Demi Oblique, Bold, Bold Oblique

Second Edition
ISBN 978-988-17328-8-0

Printed and bound in China

We would like to thank all the designers and companies who have involved in the compilation of this book. This project would not have been accomplished without their significant contribution to the production of this book. We would also like to express our gratitude to all the producers for their invaluable opinions and assistance throughout this entire project. The successful completion also owes a great deal to many professionals in the creative industry who have given us precious insights and comments. And to the many others whose names are not credited but have made specific input in this book, we thank you for your continuous support the whole time.

We would also like to give our special thanks to Wolfgang Hartmann and Bauer Types who sponsored the typefaces we used in this book as well as the text and visual materials for the preface.